Inquiry in the Classroom: Creating It, Encouraging It, Enjoying it

DAVID WRAY

Pippin Publishing

Copyright © 1999 by Pippin Publishing Corporation
Suite 232, 85 Ellesmere Road
Toronto, Ontario
M1R 4B9

Edited by Anne Fullerton
Designed by John Zehethofer
Printed and bound in Canada by Friesens

Canadian Cataloguing in Publication Data

Wray, David, 1950-
    Inquiry in the classroom: creating it, encouraging it, enjoying it

(The Pippin teacher's library; 31)
ISBN 0-88751-098-1

1. Project method in teaching. I. Title. II. Series.

LB1027.43.W72 1998   372.13'6   C98-932602-0

ISBN 0-88751-098-1

10   9   8   7   6   5   4   3   2   1

CONTENTS

. . . .

INTRODUCTION

The aim of this book is to offer practical advice to elementary school teachers wishing to adopt a project-based approach to their students' learning. In project work (sometimes also called *integrated study* or *thematic work*), areas of study are defined not according to traditional curriculum boundaries but as ways of gaining insights into particular topics or phenomena. Students investigate topics such as "Houses," "Transportation," "The Sea," or "Communications," and during the course of this study naturally engage in activities that might otherwise be classified as language arts, science, social studies, and so on.

This approach has been used for many years, and there is now a wealth of accumulated ideas about the possibilities of, strategies for, and pitfalls in project-based teaching. At its best, it involves students in motivated, self-directed, inquiry-focused learning. The curriculum is no longer divided into rather arbitrary areas which, for the students, may have little meaning. Integration enables students to see links among curriculum areas and engages them in a seamless robe of learning. This is especially relevant to the language arts. While they are involved in a project that excites them, students naturally gain practice in reading, writing, talking, and listening, all of which are used in realistic ways to satisfy real needs.

The integrated nature of project work means that it is ideally suited to an inquiry approach to teaching. If the curriculum is planned to focus on students' actual questions (rather than on bodies of knowledge predetermined by teachers), this will inevitably involve some integration. Students simply do not ask questions which can be located purely in one curriculum area. In such a context, the teacher can adopt several roles—those of facilitator, audience, and resource provider, as well as instructor. When students themselves perceive the need to learn how to do an activity, instruction is given relevance and purpose, and is more likely to be effective.

While in theory project-based learning has great potential, especially in whole language classrooms, it does have its problems. It can result in superficial activities in which students "find out" about topics in which they have only a passing interest, largely by means of copying sections from information books. It is my belief that this situation arises only when the goals and strategies of using project methods have not been sufficiently thought through. Part of the skill of teaching using an inquiry approach is to help students focus their questions into useful guides to learning. This is often easier said than done: teachers may find the practical organization and management of inquiry-led learning difficult. This book aims to help teachers with this—first, by discussing in some detail the place of projects in a holistic curriculum and, second, by presenting a range of tried-and-tested strategies for introducing, developing, monitoring, and evaluating project work in the classroom.

The first chapter reviews possible aims for project work, particularly in terms of intended learning outcomes for students. These are classified into the familiar knowledge-skills-attitudes divisions, but particular stress is placed on the role of language and literacy skills in integrating teaching goals.

The second chapter discusses strategies by which schools and teachers using project or inquiry methods can ensure that their students experience a balanced curriculum with continuity of learning. It makes suggestions for ways teachers might build curriculum content in an ordered way into a child-centered approach to learning and teaching.

In the third chapter the planning process is discussed, and several practical strategies to make planning more coherent and effective are outlined. Various suggestions for stimulating ways of beginning projects—and thereby stimulating students' interests—are given. Particular emphasis is placed on strategies for involving children in the planning process. Such a negotiated approach to classroom work is extremely important in developing independent learners.

Although a project approach properly concentrates on the processes of students' learning, it is facilitated by a clear specification of the outcomes toward which students are working. The fourth chapter makes several suggestions for possible project end products and discusses the importance of working with a specific audience in mind.

The fifth chapter examines the range of roles the teacher might adopt at various times during project work. Particular emphasis is placed on strategies for ensuring students' involvement in planning and monitoring their own work.

In the final chapter several strategies for evaluating a piece of project work and the resulting learning are discussed. Included are suggestions for making evaluation as natural a part of teaching as possible, for involving the students in evaluating their own learning, and for keeping portfolio-based records of students' achievements and learning.

. . . .

THE AIMS OF PROJECT
WORK

Teachers who are considering adopting a project approach in their classrooms will need to be able to justify their teaching methods. In classic educational terminology, they will need to determine carefully their aims and objectives. It is possible to put forward a powerful argument as to why teachers should use project work, expressed in terms of the benefits this form of teaching has for children. This chapter describes some of these benefits and thereby provides a rationale for project teaching.

Aims and objectives are, of course, only part of the story. If these are not translated into workable classroom reality, then not much has been gained. The practical issues involved in teaching through project work are considered in subsequent chapters that give guidance on how teachers may best achieve the aims and objectives discussed here.

Building on Children's Interests

The most common advice given to preservice or beginning teachers concerned about how to manage the lively youngsters over whom they have been given responsibility is "Get them interested." This can also be seen as a predominant aim of project methods.

Everybody knows that children who are interested in what they are doing are much less likely to give their teacher problems of control and discipline. It is bored children who cause trouble. What is known less well is that interested children, as well as behaving better, also learn better. Of course, it is possible to learn something without being really interested in it, as anyone knows who has studied particular facts simply because of an upcoming test. But this tends to be merely rote learning and is not of very great duration. Learning things in which you are interested, however, is much easier and tends to last longer. This simple fact explains the phenomenal memory of young children when it comes to such things as dinosaur names.

Elementary school teachers, on the whole, are a very privileged group. They deal with children who are, by their nature, interested in all sorts of things. Most have not reached the stage of adolescence when it becomes a matter of principle to express no interest in things encountered in school. Elementary children are generally fairly easy to interest in things that are worthy of interest. This fact is of major importance and underpins the project approach. If teachers can harness or channel children's interest, then a whole series of things can be learned that might otherwise have caused problems.

Just to give a small example of this, take the simple skill of using knowledge of alphabetical order to find items in a dictionary, directory, or encyclopedia. This seems a minor thing to us because we can do it, but we only have to consider the time it saves to realize its importance. Many teachers will testify that there are plenty of children who find it a difficult skill to master. There are lots of exercises in published workbooks that claim to teach the skill, and countless children dutifully go through these exercises. Unfortunately for many of them, it seems to make little difference. Yet there are other children who are never made to do the exercises but who pick up the skill simply by using encyclopedias or dictionaries to find out about things in which they are interested. They learn the skill as a byproduct of their interest in a particular topic. If we are honest as we look back, we'll probably remember that this is how we learned it also.

This is the best justification of all for using the project approach. By focusing children's work on a topic in which they are either interested to begin with or in which their interest can be stimulated, a whole range of knowledge, concepts, skills, and attitudes can be developed a good deal more painlessly than by direct teaching. What this range might encompass is discussed in the next sections.

Developing Knowledge and Concepts

THE PROBLEM WITH FACTS

Most project work results in children knowing more about a topic than they did before the work began. This is entirely natural and desirable. What is problematic, though, is specifying that an increased knowledge of facts should be an aim for project work. This does tend to happen and reflects the great emphasis education places on factual knowledge. Many people judge the quality of their education by the amount of knowledge they have and, indeed, this tends to be the focus in examinations.

There are signs, fortunately, that this over-concern with facts may be on the wane. The reasons for this shift in emphasis are not hard to find. We live in the age of the "information explosion." The amount of knowledge we have collectively about our world—and beyond—is increasing so rapidly that it is virtually impossible to select the facts that we consider vital for children to learn and remember through their schooling. Any selection is arguable. Furthermore, as all teachers know, children forget very quickly most of the facts they learn, unless, as argued earlier, they themselves see those facts as of vital interest. It seems, then, that there may not be too many facts that are essential for children to learn in elementary school. If we focus on facts that interest them, they may at least remember what they learn.

Lessening our emphasis on the teaching of facts does not, of course, mean that we can have no cognitive aims for project work. These aims, rather, should be concerned with developing children's understanding of concepts as opposed to their factual knowledge. As we shall see in a later chapter, project work can incorporate concepts from every area of the elementary curriculum, so that they do not remain fixed within one subject but can be broadened and enriched by being applied in several areas at once. A concept such as cause and effect, for example, may have one set of implications in science but quite a different set in history. The development of children's appreciation of this concept will be enriched by its treatment across the curriculum. When planning particular projects teachers will need to define the concepts they are aiming to develop, bearing in mind the curriculum areas their projects will emphasize and their students' abilities.

The message so far has been that developing understanding of concepts is of far more importance than teaching facts. It is, however, important to realize that this is only true from the teacher's point of view. The children doing the project will have a completely different view of the process and completely different objectives. Children will not respond very positively if told that the reasons they are doing a particular project are to develop their appreciation of causality and their abilities to use investigative skills! They will respond better if told they are going to be finding out about the building of the railways. The point is that the idea of developing concepts is far too abstract for children to appreciate; they are actually more interested in acquiring facts. It is this thirst for information which is at the heart of the interest I earlier argued is so important to the success of project work. This is not to say that children will not be interested and excited at the idea of doing things, whether producing a collage or preparing their own video. But "learning interesting stuff" will always be high on the list of what makes school worthwhile for an elementary student.

Here we have a real clash between teacher and children about the purposes for doing project work. The resolution of this clash demands a good deal of diplomacy from the teacher. There is no reason that we cannot explain to children why we want them to engage in a particular piece of project work, but we have to make very sure that they are getting something from the activity as well. In other words, we have to teach the things *we* consider important through the activities they consider important.

This demands a particular kind of negotiation in the classroom with which most teachers may not be very familiar. It implies that we are willing to explain to children why we want them to do certain things, and also that we are prepared to modify the activities we ask them to do in the light of their reaction to them. The idea of negotiation is discussed further in a later chapter.

Developing Skills

There is a whole range of important skills that can be developed through project work. For some of these, project work may be the only place in the elementary curriculum where they are covered. But all the skills discussed in what follows are likely to be developed more effectively through activities that children see as purposeful. It is possible to teach these skills through specific exercises, but the danger of poor learning and inadequate transfer is always there. Project work does give a meaningful and real context for learning, with more possibility for lasting effect.

INVESTIGATION SKILLS

Most projects should include some form of first-hand experience for the children, through which investigation skills can be developed. This experience may be outside the classroom—for example, a visit to an interesting site—or it may take place inside the classroom as children handle objects or investigate physical phenomena. Following are brief descriptions of some of the specific investigation skills that can be part of project work.

Observation. Children can be extremely bad at noticing and looking closely at things. Their abilities can be developed if they are given specific tasks that involve these activities. This demands preparation so that children will be alert to exactly what they are looking for. To give just one example, the project may involve a visit to a local woodland. One group of children could be asked to focus specifically on the various small animals they will see. They could look at pictures beforehand and discuss what they are likely to find. Teachers could suggest that, during the visit, students might keep a log of what they see, noting any features that may enable them to identify the animals later. They may also make sketches or more detailed drawings where appropriate.

Identification. Children also need to be shown how to give names to what they observe. This involves matching features they notice with those described in other sources, and may mean using specific apparatus such as identification keys. In the woodland project example, the children could try to match their descriptions of the animals they observed with those given in reference books on small mammals, birds, and insects. This matching activity will proceed with whatever degree of subtlety the children are capable of. With the younger ones it may simply be about color and shape, but older children will be able to use more sophisticated criteria.

Classification. Classifying phenomena into types is an important element of investigation, and children need to be taught to pick out relationships among the various things they observe. In the woodland project, the children could be encouraged to sort the animals they observed into sets with things in common. They may suggest several ways of doing this, perhaps beginning with color and later moving on to the number of legs.

Recording. Observations will eventually be recorded, although this aspect need not be stressed with young children. There are many ways of doing this and children need to be introduced to the possibilities of drawing, painting, and modeling, and preparing diagrams, written descriptions, tables, and so on. Each of these involves its own set of practical skills (discussed in the next section), but each also involves a decision as to its appropriateness in terms of what is to be recorded for what audience.

Explanation. An important element of investigation is explaining why phenomena are as they are. Attempting to give an explanation may be seen as a form of hypothesis production as it is necessary to take the explanation back to the phenomena to see if it always holds true. This is the basis of problem solving.

PRACTICAL SKILLS

A list of the practical skills that can be taught within the context of a project would be endless: every teacher would be able to add something different to it. However, as a starting point, the list given below may spark some ideas.

Arts and crafts. One of the most frequent end products of a class project is some form of arts and crafts, whether it be observational drawing, painting, collage, three-dimensional modeling, pottery, weaving, or so on. Most of these things will be done anyway in an industrious elementary class, but if they contribute to the presentation of a piece of project work, they give the children a meaningful purpose for acquiring and practicing the necessary skills .

Manipulating special equipment. Magnifying lenses, microscopes, audiorecorders, slide viewers, videocameras, computers, overhead projectors, and so on all have their place within the classroom. If the children are to use them efficiently and effectively they will need opportunities to practice the necessary skills. These opportunities may, of course, arise outside of project work, and the novelty of the equipment may be such that children will clamor to learn to use it regardless of the context. They will, however, really appreciate the technology when it is being used for some clearly identifiable purpose, and project work is the most likely place for this to happen.

Presenting information. Presenting information in a form appropriate to its nature and intended audience is an aspect of information and study skills, and will be dealt with in the next section. But there is a practical element to this which can be considered here. Children need a range of practical skills in order to present information in effective ways, including the ability to write legibly and to use a keyboard. They may also profitably learn to bind their work into a book, and acquire from their teacher a knowledge, however rudimentary, of effective display techniques. Again, a project gives a real purpose to these things.

INFORMATION AND STUDY SKILLS

The area of information skills is one in which project work has a unique contribution to make. Finding and extracting information from appropriate sources is what most projects are about, and these often-neglected skills can be developed in contexts which the children see as real. Weaknesses in these skills tend to manifest themselves quite clearly. Children who leaf through reference books page by page hoping to find what they are looking for by chance, children whose project work consists of sections copied word for word from these reference books, and children who, after the project is done, cannot actually tell you much about what they have learned or written in their work all need to develop information skills.

The six types of skills identified in what follows are described in terms of what a ten- or eleven-year-old child might be able to do. Teachers need to decide how far along the way to achieving these things their particular students can be led. It is important, however, that teachers realize that children of any age can be introduced to information skills as long as it is done in an appropriate way.

Defining the subject and purpose. This involves specifying what information is required and why. It implies more than the vague "I want to find out about..." which seems all too common in elementary school project work. Children need to be encouraged to specify as precisely as possible what it is they want to find out, and what they will do with that information when they have found it. They may be asked to draw up a list of questions to which they want to find answers.

Locating information. This includes knowing how to use the library system to track down likely sources of the information required and how to find information efficiently in books and other sources, including on-line services and databases. Computers are extremely useful tools for finding information, but not unless the children possess the requisite skills for using them. Besides these media, children need to learn how to use the most important information resource—other people. Asking the right questions is an important skill in which even many adults are insufficiently practiced.

Selecting information. This means choosing the information required to meet the purpose identified earlier. Children often find it very difficult to be selective in the information they extract from books in particular, often resorting to wholesale copying of long passages that may bear on a topic in broad terms but have no relevance to the specific question at hand. They need to be shown how to match their particular information requirements to what is available, and how to take note of information rather than copy it. Drawing up a list of specific questions will certainly help them in this, as they will then have to note down answers to these questions rather than transcribing everything the book says.

Organizing information. This means synthesizing the information found into a full answer to the original question. Pulling together information from a range of sources can be a very demanding task. It is, however, made a good deal easier if the information needed is defined very precisely, as suggested earlier. Children must be encouraged to consult a range of information sources in their quest, and then to look for common points or instances of disagreement.

Evaluating information. Children should be encouraged to evaluate the accuracy, relevance, and source of the information found. Children naturally tend to believe, as do many adults, that everything they read is true. The teacher may need to confront students with examples of incorrect or biased information if a questioning attitude is to be developed. Possibilities for this include out-of-date books, biased newspaper reports, and advertising material.

Communicating results. This may involve either using the information for personal purposes or presenting it to others. In the latter case, children should be encouraged to define an audience for their finished work and actually present it to that audience. They can then assess the work's appropriateness for their audience by observing the reaction to it. The obvious example is having older children prepare information booklets for younger children in the same school, although there are many other possibilities.

It is possible to see all teaching as being concerned with the development of communication skills. Communication involves chiefly, but not exclusively, the language arts—that is, speaking and listening (oracy), reading, and writing. We have certainly become familiar with the idea of developing language across the whole curriculum. Yet it is still probably true that most of the work children are expected to do with the aim of developing communication skills is done for its own sake, rather than with any express purpose in mind. This is not necessarily always bad. There is a place for the language exercise, if not such a prominent place as it often is given. But the whole range of communication skills can be practiced within the context of a project without resorting to exercises at all.

Oracy. It is perhaps self-evident that developing children's abilities to speak clearly and appropriately is easier if they have something to speak about, and developing their abilities to listen attentively and with understanding is easier if there is something worth listening to. Project work can provide both of these opportunities. During a project, children may be involved in asking people questions, interviewing, listening to tape-recordings, telling and listening to stories, telling the rest of the class about their work, cooperating in small group discussions, and taking part in improvised drama. All these activities will develop their oral abilities but will also, from the children's point of view, advance their work on a project that interests them.

Reading. During a project children receive a great deal of reading practice almost without being aware of it. This may include reading reference books, stories, letters, advertisements, instructions, newspapers, and wall charts, as well as other children's writing. In fact, over several projects, just about every form of reading imaginable can be covered. This is a good deal more than is usually possible if the main reading that children do is confined to their basals.

Writing. The picture is the same with writing. There is, within project work, a great deal of scope for practice in most forms of writing. Children can write stories, poems, descriptive pieces, and personal reactions. They can give reports, present arguments, and record observations and speculations. They can write for particular audiences in particular formats, and can be encouraged to draft and revise what they write. They can use pens, pencils, typewriters, and word-processors. And all this vast experience can be provided with a real purpose in mind: that of presenting some interesting work students have done so that their friends, classmates, or others can share it. This is a good deal broader and more purposeful than the very common experience of working from books of exercises, however well thought out these may be.

Developing Attitudes

Any classroom experience affects children's attitudes toward school and learning. This is a truism. Unfortunately there are many cases of children whose experience in classrooms results in them forming very negative attitudes to the whole business. Nobody would claim that project work was a complete panacea for this, yet it is true that engaging children's interests in what they do at school has more chance of developing positive attitudes than does ignoring those interests. And this, as was suggested earlier, is where project work's main strength lies. It can have benefits in four main areas.

POSITIVE ATTITUDES TO LEARNING

If we ask ourselves why negative attitudes toward learning develop, we might attribute most of the blame to two major causes. First, what school seems to count as appropriate material to learn may not coincide with a child's interests and, second, a child's experiences of school may include more failure than success, which comes to color that child's whole perception of the process. Project work can work against both of these situations. There are very few children, at least in the elementary grades, whose interest is impossible to stimulate if enough effort and care are taken. And once this interest is captured, then all kinds of surprising benefits can flow. Getting children to want to know about something is the major part of the battle.

We also need to be alert to the very negative effects experienced by children who perceive themselves to be failures. The corollary of the old maxim "Nothing succeeds like success" is that "Nothing fails like failure." Project work, again, can operate against this because it is possible, in a cooperative piece of work, for every child's contribution to be valued, and thus for every child to succeed to some degree. This, of course, demands some sensitive handling by the teacher. It is clearly not sensible to suggest that a child who excels at making collages but not much else should simply do this during every project. But there is scope in a project, particularly if it is a group undertaking, for each student to contribute to and take pride in well-produced work that will often go beyond his or her individual capabilities. In project work, the whole is often greater than the sum of its parts.

CURIOSITY

Most young children are naturally curious about the world they live in. Sadly, for many of them, this will not be particularly encouraged either at home or at school, and a great deal of potential will thereby be lost. Teachers need to find ways of encouraging curiosity and the desire to enquire into and to investigate. It would be very difficult to find an activity in the elementary curriculum more suited to this than project work. This, by its very nature, revolves around "finding out," and children participating in it can indeed make discoveries. It should be noted, however, that if this is to work it demands a certain approach to the activity. What it does not imply is that the teacher does all the thinking ahead of the children. This often seems to happen, with the result that, far from developing curiosity, all the children do is complete a series of teacher-devised worksheets. Clearly the teacher does need to do some preplanning if the project is to be successful, but there must be scope left for children to follow their own leads.

INDEPENDENCE

It is often said that one of the aims of teachers is to make themselves redundant. This implies that we should be encouraging children to make decisions and take actions without always having to consult us. If we are working toward the goal of child independence, it can readily be seen again that there is little real benefit in teachers doing all the planning in project work. Children should be involved. If we do not let them make independent decisions, how will they ever learn to do so? In project work there is scope for them to develop their own lines of interest, to specify their own purposes, to find their own resources, and to decide how to present their own work. Of course, the teacher should not just opt out of helping. All children need some assistance, and the younger the children, the greater the guidance they will need. But, wherever possible, the teacher should move toward being a guide, rather than the source of all the answers.

COOPERATION

Most teachers recognize the benefits to be had when children are encouraged to cooperate in their work in all curriculum areas. They learn from discussion, from sharing, from listening, and from contributing their part to something larger. Project work is an ideal activity in which this kind of learning through cooperating can take place. Groups of children can work together with a single purpose to produce a joint piece of work. One of the criticisms that is often leveled at group work in elementary schools is that it is not really group work at all but rather just children sitting close together doing the same work. This problem arises simply because the nature of the task they are asked to do is more important to children than their seating arrangements or any exhortations to collaborate their teacher may give them. If their task is basically an individual one then they will not cooperate in any meaningful sense. In project work, of course, the group task can be defined to require cooperation, with the resultant beneficial effects.

Aiming High

It is inevitable that any discussion of aims and objectives becomes fairly lofty. This is not necessarily a fault. Teaching would be a dull and sad affair if we were not allowed to have grandiose aims for what we do. We ought to have a reasonable idea of where we are going in any kind of teaching, and that place ought to be somewhere worth going to.

Aims, though essential, are only a small part of the story, however. It is necessary to supplement them with some practical help concerning how to travel along the road. The next chapters concentrate on offering this practical guidance.

. . . .

CURRICULUM COVERAGE

AND CONTINUITY

"Miss Beale said you would show me round, to look at the projects," said Andrew. "Why, do you want to copy one?" asked Victor.... "You could copy mine, only someone might recognise it. I've done that three times already." "Whatever for?" said Andrew. "Don't you get tired of it?" Victor shook his head and his hair. "That's only once a year. I did that two times at the junior school and now I'm doing that again," he said. "I do fish, every time. Fish are easy. They're all the same shape."

Jan Mark, *Thunder and Lightnings*, Puffin Books, 1977

Many teachers would somewhat guiltily admit to recognizing Victor's description of the experience of project work. One of the major problems that has been identified in respect to project work is that of curriculum continuity. Students may move from a topic on the ancient Egyptians to one on the sea, without much thought being given to progression in their learning. Clearly this problem is a real one. If project work is to fulfill some of its great promise, continuity and curriculum coverage need to be given some consideration.

What Is the Elementary School Curriculum?

Debates about the content of the curriculum have filled many books and journals in the past and no doubt will continue to do so. Nevertheless, what is more remarkable than many people have admitted is the degree of consensus there appears to be among teachers and schools, even across national boundaries, about the content of the elementary school curriculum. All elementary schools give major attention to the teaching of reading, to students' use of spoken and written language, and to mathematics;

they also recognize the value of such things as science, the study of social and environmental topics, physical education, and experience of arts and crafts. More recently, practically every elementary school has acknowledged the importance of familiarization with microcomputers and has begun to make them available for students' use.

There is, of course, major debate about how these things should be taught, and about the amount of time that should be devoted to each of them. Although greater conformity in allocation of class time is perhaps desirable, it is extremely unlikely that any rigid rules could be imposed on teachers concerning how they are to teach the elements of a curriculum, if for no other reason than the sheer diversity of teaching methods being used at the moment.

One of the major areas of debate about the elementary school curriculum, which concerns very much the role of project work within it, has been the issue of integration. On one side of the argument are those who believe that the curriculum can be treated as a collection of subjects; on the other are those who see it in terms of a seamless robe of learning. Most teachers now accept that rigid subject divisions are artificial for elementary school students and do not reflect the way young children see the world. Many, however, are wary of abandoning subject divisions entirely because of their concerns about external pressures and demands for standards.

Project work can fit into either side of the integration argument. Projects can be planned so that the whole of the work done by a class relates, for a time, to the project being undertaken. They can also be planned so that at different times during the week, the students study historical aspects of the project, geographical aspects, scientific aspects, and so on. Or the project can be planned to include work in some subject areas only, leaving the rest to be treated at separate times. Which of these approaches is taken tends to reflect an individual teacher's feeling about curriculum integration and its feasibility. It must not be forgotten, however, that to teach using project methods at all implies a certain acceptance of the concept of an integrated curriculum. Any method of approaching a project aims to get students to see links among the various pieces of work they do, in an attempt to remove some of the artificiality. As I suggested in an earlier chapter, teaching through projects is essentially a holistic activity.

So the debate in project work will not be about whether the curriculum should be integrated, but rather to what extent. To clarify the issues underlying this question, we need to look at some of the possibilities for placing project work in the curriculum.

Project Work within the Curriculum

The first decision that teachers need to make is whether project work is to be thought of as a basic or an extra. Many teachers tend to see the curriculum in terms of "skills and frills"—that is, as composed of certain essential parts and other less essential, more informal parts. The former generally consist of the three R's and the latter of subjects such as art, physical education, environmental studies, and so on. Some teachers will see project work as an opportunity to teach "basic" subjects in a more meaningful and interesting way, and it will itself become a basic part of their curriculum. Others will see it as an extra and an opportunity to motivate students to practice basic skills which have been taught elsewhere. Others will still see it as a motivating extra, but will deliberately structure the project and their basic skills work so that these complement each other. These three approaches will result in different ways of planning and executing project work.

BASIC SKILLS LEARNING

The integrated approach. In this approach the teacher uses the project as a vehicle for the teaching of basic skills. This is done because it is felt that such skills can only really be learned if the students see for themselves that they are useful, and if they are set in a practical, purposeful context from the very beginning. A possible objection to this approach concerns the incidental nature of such teaching and the possibility that opportunities to teach certain skills may not occur naturally. This may lead to certain areas being missed or insufficiently developed.

This objection can be countered by taking two initial precautions. First, a program for the teaching of basic skills can be drawn up, which can help to ensure full coverage over time. This program is likely to be more effective if it is planned on a whole-school basis and if it is accompanied by some form of record keeping. Second, in the implementation of this approach, extra basic skills teaching can be planned, both to "top up" what is done through the project and to cover areas that may not be possible to integrate.

An example will help to clarify the approach. In a project entitled "Vacations" with a mixed class of nine- to eleven-year-olds, the teacher drew up a list of "basic" skills she hoped could be taught during the project. When planning the project in collaboration with the students, she made certain that they included in the plans activities in which these skills would be exercised. These skills and their corresponding activities were as follows:

— *Reading for details*
Reading reference books and travel brochures for details of specific resorts and countries; reading brochures for details of vacation prices and terms (reading the small print); reading passport applications.

— *Reading critically*
Reading brochures and other publicity material and trying to determine the truth about resorts and hotels, etc.

— *Surveying books and other written materials*
Checking a variety of written materials to ascertain whether they contain information useful at that point; using the contents and index pages of books; skimming printed materials quickly.

— *Using reference books and encyclopedias*
Looking for information about countries and cities in the world, specifically their tourist attractions; finding out about various vacation pursuits (canoeing, swimming, windsurfing, etc.).

— *Using telephone directories*
Finding phone numbers and addresses of local travel agents; finding suppliers of certain travel goods.

— *Writing letters*
Writing to tourist offices to request information.

— *Writing narrative*
Writing accounts of vacations, real and imaginary.

— *Writing to persuade*
Writing brochures to advertise particular resorts.

— *Writing to describe*
Writing descriptions of resorts, vacation activities, and experiences.

— *Writing personally*
Writing personal reactions to places visited on vacation or experiences had.

— *Reading and making maps*
Using maps of the world and ordnance survey maps to locate countries and resorts, and to plan routes; making

maps of various scales to show places visited and written about.

— *Measuring distances and using scale*
Working out distances to and between resorts on maps, using map scales.
— *Performing calculations with money*
Working out the cost of a family vacation by using various brochures; working out deposits, insurance expenses, and travel costs.
— *Using timetables*
Working out travel times for journeys to various resorts using rail, bus, and airline schedules.

When students were engaged in these activities, the teacher took the opportunity to instruct them directly in the appropriate skills, using as a starting point the project materials. She felt, however, that there were skill areas missing from this work, so the following were given teaching time independent of the project:

— *Reading for pleasure*
A daily half-hour of uninterrupted silent sustained reading.
— *Extra basic reading help for those with difficulties*
Using their usual reading materials, although several lessons were given based on reading material from the project.
— *Basic mathematics computational practice*
Using the usual mathematics materials in the school.
— *Science work*
Concentrating on water, which seemed as near to "Vacations" as could be achieved!

The sequential approach. In this approach project work is seen as an opportunity for students to put to purposeful use the basic skills they have already been taught. Project work, therefore, has to follow basic skills work and thus be separate from it.

This approach has several implications. First, because basic skills teaching is given separate and distinct time by the teacher, the students will readily sense that this is the work that the teacher really considers to be most important. They will begin to pick up the message that project work is less important, and hence less worthy of real effort. The teacher will have to work very hard to get them to see it as a vital and interesting activity, which is how they must perceive it if the aim of providing a motivating context in which to practice basic skills is to be realized. Paradoxically, if the basic skills are taught in isolation, they risk being perceived by the students as activities they must do only because their teacher has told them to. They know the teacher thinks they are important, but the students view them as meaningless because they have no context.

Finally, because in this system there is necessarily a gap between the teaching of a skill and its use in a project, there is a danger that, by the time they come to the project, students will have forgotten the skills. Even more likely, they may not be able to transfer the skills from one context to another. This is very common indeed. It is seen at its starkest when students spend long periods learning spellings for a test, only to misspell the very same words when writing a story. Students who can successfully complete any number of exercises on study skills may forget all this when they come to use reference materials in earnest in their projects. Transfer of learning can be a real problem.

Because of these inherent problems, it is unlikely that the sequential approach will satisfy the aims of those who try it or be an effective use of project work. The compromise described below may be welcomed by those who wish to avoid these problems but feel hesitant about adopting the all-or-nothing integrated approach.

The concurrent approach. In this approach an attempt is made to teach basic skills alongside their use in project work. This allows the skills to be taught systematically and in the structured way many teachers are familiar with. It also allows students to have opportunities to use the skills in real contexts and for real purposes as they are being taught, thus avoiding the problems of students forgetting or being unable to transfer skills.

An example of this approach will make it clearer. In a project on "Airplanes" with a class of seven- and eight-year-olds, the teacher decided that the students would need to use the following skills:

— reading to pick out the main ideas
— summarizing in their own words
— handling reference books (using the contents page)
— writing to communicate information
— arranging in order of size
— drawing to scale

The activity in the project for which these skills were required was the production by student groups of their own booklets about "Famous Airplanes." This work involved them in finding information about various airplanes in reference books, noting down the main points about each one, and putting this together to write a page or two about each plane. When this was done, they were to arrange the planes their group had studied in order of length, attach a drawing of each on roughly the same scale, and make up their booklet, which would then be displayed for the rest of the class to read.

The teacher began with some work with the class on using reference books to find information. He did two or three lessons on this, finishing each with exercises for the students to do in groups and by themselves. Next he introduced the class to the reference books on airplanes he had collected and did a series of group lessons (because there were not enough books for the whole class) on their use. The students were then given the task of finding and reading the book sections on the planes they wished to study.

While they were doing this in their groups, alongside other normal class work the teacher introduced some work on note taking. After several exercises on this he began to ask the groups to note down things they found interesting about the airplanes they were researching. The next step was to get them to write from their notes, and this similarly was introduced and practiced by the whole class before being done as part of the project. The project continued like this, with skills being introduced and practiced, as far as possible, by the class, before being used as part of the project.

While this approach may seem to combine the best of both worlds, having both structure and purpose, it does demand a great deal of forethought and planning. It is unlikely that approaching every project like this could be sustained for long. In any case, students differ in their rate of picking up new skills, and the class teaching elements described in this example will quickly become ineffective. This will enforce a more individualized or small group approach, which adds to the complexity. However, this approach does have much to commend it, and it is certainly recommended if the teacher finds it feasible.

CURRICULUM BALANCE

Many investigations into practice in elementary schools have shown a wide divergence in the amount of time devoted to various curriculum areas. Mathematics, for example, may be given anywhere from 3 to 12 hours per week in different classes, and other curriculum areas show similar variation. If we accept that students can only learn what they are given an opportunity to learn, there is clearly a case for attempting some standardization of curriculum time, even though we would wish to leave something to the teacher's discretion. Individual teachers need to provide a balanced curriculum for all their students.

Project work may take up a large slice of time in an elementary class, and its impact on curriculum balance must be considered. This is a little difficult to assess because of the integrated nature of most project work, but the teacher should make some attempt to weigh up how much of the work of particular projects is devoted to the various curriculum areas.

In order to do this, an initial judgment needs to be made about what the curriculum areas are. This can be a very difficult issue since there is no complete consensus among the many analyses that have been published in a variety of sources. As a starting point, the diagram may be useful to teachers. It begins with the idea of four basic curriculum areas as listed on the left, and subdivides these as you move to the right. Teachers can decide for themselves exactly how far they wish to subdivide, and then try to determine the amount of time likely to be spent by students on each area during an average week's work on their current project. To these figures add the time devoted specifically to the areas elsewhere in the week. This will give a rough and ready measure of current curriculum time allocation. (Note that as typical a week as possible should be chosen for analysis.) It is then up to the individual teacher to decide whether this allocation is desirable and fits within school or school board curriculum guidelines.

If a fair balance is not achieved, we need to consider what can be done. There are strategies for handling imbalance, relating particularly to project work:

1. Check whether it is possible to alleviate the imbalance by adjusting the time given to various areas outside of project work. This may involve replacing a language session with a math session or planning a regular science session, for example.
2. Is it possible to add extra dimensions to the project work to make up for lack of coverage of certain areas? Is it possible, for example, to think of some way of bringing math work into the project (always bearing in mind the dangers of artificiality discussed earlier)?

Language	reading	learning to read reading to learn reading for pleasure

	writing	writing for various
		   purposes
		writing for various
		   audiences
		secretarial skills

	oral work	speaking listening discussion

Mathematics	number	using concrete
		   experiences
		developing abstract
		   ideas

	shape	two dimensional three dimensional
	practical	measurement investigations
Discovery	environmental	local geography world geography investigations
	social	history social studies religious studies
	scientific	experiments observations recording
Creative Arts	art	drawing painting
	crafts	clay work needlecraft
	music	listening music making
	drama	mime improvisation
	physical education	gymnastics games

3. Make a note that in the next project done by the class certain areas may need to be at the forefront so as to compensate for their lack of coverage at present. Thus a science-based project might be followed by a literature-based project. Balance may be achieved over a whole semester or year, rather than every week.

Building on Learning across the Years

As noted at the beginning of this chapter, continuity can often be a problem in a curriculum that emphasizes project work. It is certainly an issue to be considered, but we should avoid seeing it in too simple a way. Because a child repeats a project in two different years, this does not necessarily mean that the second time around is time wasted. The concept of the "spiral curriculum" suggests that similar topics can be studied at various stages in the education process, with students gaining fresh insights and a fresh depth of understanding on each occasion. To repeat something, if this means to reconsider and extend it, can be a very valuable learning experience for students. Consequently, simplistic views about continuity, which specify suitable content for particular age groups, may actually work against potentially useful learning.

The approach of specifying suitable project titles for particular age groups has become a popular response to the problem of continuity. It often results in lists similar to the one following, which was taken from the agreed curriculum guidelines of an elementary school in the north of England.

- *six- and seven-year-olds*: animals, homes, our street, prehistoric animals
- *seven- and eight-year-olds*: early man, farming, shops, the sea
- *eight- and nine-year-olds*: explorers, people who help us, water, our town, the Romans
- *nine- and ten-year-olds*: food, weather, communications, space, the Normans, air
- *ten- and eleven-year-olds*: Europe, the Elizabethans, transportation, our bodies, the Victorians

A list such as this, distributed schoolwide, has the advantage of alerting staff so that suitable resources for each project can be centralized and ideas for development can be passed on from teacher to teacher. Furthermore, if the list is a product of detailed staff discussion and is rethought regularly, it can be a useful means of ensuring continuity. However, it does have several inherent problems:

1. Students may not get the opportunity to develop and extend their learning in certain areas over periods longer than the duration of a single project. Thus their learning through projects risks becoming like a series of snapshots, which are difficult to relate one to another.
2. By concentrating on project titles, there is a risk that project work will come to emphasize factual knowledge over processes of learning and skills. The problems with this were discussed in the previous chapter.
3. By specifying titles for projects, teachers' enthusiasms and initiative are made to take second place to a predetermined plan. Teachers may find several of the titles suggested for their age group unstimulating, and nothing will more quickly make work seem boring to students than a teacher who is bored.
4. Finally, and perhaps most important, the system does not allow for students' interests, or for events that may occur without warning yet still provide scope for wonderful projects.

To achieve continuity in project work, there seem to be two alternative approaches to the predetermined list of titles.

Record keeping. If teachers keep records of the projects that individual students have done in their class, then these can be passed to the next teacher, along with samples of work from each project, if possible. The new teacher then has a basis on which to decide whether to use completely new topics for project work or to build on work the students have done in the past. Thus, continuity can be achieved without rigid prescription.

Mapping objectives. This second alternative sees continuity more in terms of developing skills and concepts than in covering content. There has been much debate over the feasibility of mapping out series of objectives that students are expected to achieve by certain ages. If objectives are seen in terms of skills and concepts, the approach has its attractions. By means of such a list of objectives teachers can know what skills and concepts to concentrate on with their classes, and what things to evaluate and record. Continuity depends to a large extent on the sequential development of skills and concepts, and without guidelines it is difficult to see how teachers can ensure their students are making progress rather than marking time or regressing.

There are, however, several problems with this approach that need further discussion. First, a list of specified objectives can be perceived as a straitjacket. There is, though, no such thing as the perfectly average class or child, and consequently any set of objectives must be at least partially inappropriate for any group of students. The most important factor in what any teacher can achieve with a class is, of course, the students themselves, and they will largely determine the feasibility of attaining any prespecified objectives. Thus, in any given class, there may be students who will be able to achieve more than is anticipated for them, and there will certainly be those for whom the objectives are overly ambitious. The teacher will need constantly to readjust expectations in the light of experience with particular students.

Furthermore, appropriate objectives will vary from school to school, and no single set will fit exactly the needs and potential of any two schools. Because of this, it is essential that lists of objectives be tailored to particular schools. The only way for this to happen is for staff members at each school to work together to devise their own, even if they use a list from elsewhere as a starting point. The discussion this involves has, of course, important effects in its own right as a staff-development exercise.

It is also important to see objectives not so much in terms of end products but of processes with which students should have experience. The process-product debate has a long history in education, and the concept of objectives for learning has tended to be seen in product terms. When objectives are seen as relating to processes, however, they may be phrased in terms such as "Students should have experience of using a book to search for information," rather than "Students should be able to use a book to search for information." The latter phrasing does not specify any particular conditions under which this should be judged, such as the difficulty of the book, the motivation of the child, the purpose of the exercise, etc., all of which can affect the child's ability to do the task. It would, therefore, be extremely difficult to say that a child had achieved this objective. Yet it is not difficult to say that a child has had experience of something, without having to make dubious judgments about the success of this experience.

Finally, objectives do not provide teaching material in their own right. A danger in specifying objectives is that teachers might feel they have to teach these directly. This can lead to teaching that has little real relevance for the students. Any teaching needs to be set in a meaningful context if it is to be fully effective. Thus objectives should inform teaching rather than determine it.

If these points are borne in mind, it is possible for specifications of objectives to offer teachers useful guidelines. As an example of such a specification, the figure contains the objectives list used by one school of seven- to eleven-year-old children. The means whereby this list was produced are important. Teachers in the school wanted to develop some guidelines about the aspects of study or information skills they should concentrate on with each age group. After several whole staff and working group meetings, the list of objectives was agreed upon. It was introduced in their school curriculum policy documents with the following sentence: "These are the aspects of information-handling skills which the *average* child should get some experience in during a particular year at school." These teachers were very aware that some of their students would not be able to achieve the objectives for their age group, whereas others would be able to move well past them.

The Handling of Information

By the end of the school year, 7- and 8-year-olds should have had experience of
   — putting words into alphabetical order using the first letter
   — using the first letter to find a word in a dictionary or encyclopedia
   — using a simple dictionary to check the meaning of a word, or its spelling
   — finding a book on a particular subject by searching the shelves
   — using features of the book such as title, cover, and publisher's blurb to determine the subject
   — using the contents page to locate specific chapters
   — reading for main ideas, e.g. reading a chapter in order to give it a title
   — finding specific facts in a book by scanning
   — writing the information gleaned from a book in their own words
   — choosing appropriate pictures to illustrate what has been found out from books

By the end of the school year, 8- and 9-year-olds should have had experience of
   — consolidation of previous year's skills
   — using second and third letters to put words in alphabetical order

- finding words in dictionaries or encyclopedias by second or third letters
- using the volume titles of encyclopedias to find the correct volume, e.g. *Able* to *Axe*
- using guide words to find words in a dictionary or encyclopedia
- opening a dictionary at roughly the correct place to find a word
- using the subject index to find the Dewey number of a subject
- finding the shelf with the correct Dewey number and picking out a relevant book
- assessing the usefulness of a particular book by glancing through it
- using an index to find specific facts
- using a glossary to understand difficult words
- reading a book to answer specific questions
- checking the information found in one book by reading another on a similar subject
- using the information found in a book to write imaginative stories
- presenting information by charts or diagrams where appropriate
- compiling a list of books used in a particular investigation (bibliography)

By the end of the school year, 9- and 10-year-olds should have had experience of
- consolidation of previous years' skills
- using a thesaurus to find words of similar meanings
- understanding the dictionary treatment of multipart words, e.g. *football, footpump*
- using cross-references in an encyclopedia
- using features of a book such as its date to determine reliability
- making notes on a particular book, or passage, by jotting down the main ideas of paragraphs as they are read
- interpreting graphs and tables
- consulting several books on a subject before beginning to present the information gained
- presenting information in a variety of ways, including illustrated booklets, 3-D models, tape recordings, etc.

By the end of the school year, 10- and 11-year-olds should have had experience of
- consolidation of previous years' skills
- understanding the guide given to pronunciation in a dictionary
- using an adult dictionary to determine meanings and spellings of words
- using a full range of library skills to find and review relevant material

— organizing notes taken on a book or article under headings and subheadings
— synthesizing information from a variety of sources
— presenting information in the form of a reasoned argument

The main argument of this chapter has been that project work needs to be considered carefully in terms of continuity and progression in the curriculum. It is possible to achieve this through planning, some of which needs to involve the whole school staff.

. . . .

PLANNING PROJECT WORK

Clearly, if project work is to fulfill its potential as a valuable part of the elementary school curriculum, it needs to be planned very carefully indeed. This is true of any teaching activity, of course. Generally, the more carefully an activity is planned, the more likely it is to succeed, and certainly the clearer the teacher will be about exactly where things are leading and what children are learning in the process. "Yes, but...," many teachers will say at this point, "why is it that whenever I spend a long time planning something, it goes reasonably well but seems to lack sparkle, yet when I simply do something on the spur of the moment, it seems to go wonderfully well—the children are enthusiastic and produce work I didn't think they were capable of?" Maybe too much planning is not a good thing?

For a solution to this conundrum let us look more carefully at what is meant by planning.

Planning as a Framework

First, does planning necessarily mean being prepared for every eventuality in teaching, to such a degree that you are not surprised, and therefore not excited, by anything that occurs? Well, of course, it can mean this, but this is not the meaning I have in mind in this chapter. Here I shall be using the term *planning* to mean thinking out a framework for events that might happen.

Within this framework lots of exciting things might take place, with projects taking new directions as circumstances and children's responses determine. Planning should allow for novelty, or it risks becoming a straitjacket. Planning should also not be thought of as something which is only done once, at the beginning of a project. You may need to revise your planning many times during a project and, as I stress again and again in this book, include contributions from the children. This is not to say that no initial preparation is necessary. You will need to make some plans in order to capitalize on the many opportunities that project work provides for meaningful learning. It is little use spotting a wonderful opportunity for teaching a particular skill in the course of a project if this teaching has to wait until you have a chance to make or collect suitable materials. "Strike while the iron is hot" is a useful phrase to bear in mind, and this implies some work in advance.

Two points, therefore, should be to the fore when considering how to plan projects:

1. Planning involves creating a framework for possible lines of development rather than spelling out exactly where these lines should lead.
2. Planning should not be done by the teacher in isolation, but should involve the children from the very beginning.

Bearing these points in mind, the rest of this chapter will look in more detail at things to be considered when planning projects. These include possible starting points, strategies for developing ideas, ways to involve children in the process, choosing resources and planning access to them, the physical context, and the social context.

Project Starting Points

There are, of course, as many ways of starting a project as there are projects, and it is only possible to mention some of the major ones here. These include visits, visitors, television and video, and stories and poetry.

VISITS

A class field trip can be used very effectively as a stimulus for a project. The possibilities are endless and vary from the spectacular to the everyday. Some suggestions are given below, with examples of the kind of work that might be sparked by the visit.

Although field trips are described here as a starting point, this does not imply that they have to take place at the very beginning of the project. This may sometimes be appropriate, and taking children on a visit with little previous discussion can be an effective way of enthusing them, particularly the younger ones.

Almost always, however, the visit will be more successful with some preparation. This *must* be done if part of the purpose of the visit is to focus children's attention on a particular aspect or to introduce a particular task. In these cases it is the anticipation of the visit that is the real stimulus. In terms of time, preparing for the visit may, in fact, take up an equal or greater amount than the work done to follow it up.

A local farm. Children might study the kinds of animals to be found, the job of the farmer, the farming year, or the crops that are grown. They might compare different types of farms, in different parts of the country and in different countries.

The train station. The jobs of various railway workers might be studied, from engine drivers to station porters. Children could investigate the history of the railways, their local railway line, or how trains work.

The fire station. The job of fire fighters, fire-fighting techniques, and the sequence of events when a fire breaks out are all possibilities for work here.

A local park. The ecology of the park could be studied, and flora and fauna mapped and investigated. Students could measure, identify, and classify trees, make leaf and bark rubbings, and study pollution indicators.

A zoo or safari park. Animals could be studied and comparisons made between their natural and present habitats. The "ideal" zoo could be planned and mapped.

A museum. Children could design their own guide to the museum. They might also sketch or photograph exhibits to be used later for project displays.

Local sports grounds. The history of a sport or a local or national sports team could be studied. Children could write their own sports rule books, either for real or invented sports.

A shopping mall or plaza. Students could survey the types of goods on sale, map their countries of origin, and draw up tables of likes and dislikes. Particular items could be surveyed in more detail—for example, types of bread.

Factories. Industrial processes could be studied along with factory jobs. Children could interview employees about their work and research the factory's history.

Downtown. The town or city could be mapped, traffic surveyed, and passersby questioned about their destinations, with the results displayed graphically. Children could look at particular features such as traffic flow systems, the siting of various stores, etc., and suggest improvements to their design.

Mountains, rivers, lakes, forests, etc. Outdoor visits have a good deal of scope for environmental study, perhaps focusing on flora, fauna, pollution, etc. Recreational use of the countryside could be studied, and children could design their own visitors' booklets.

Visitors from outside school can be a useful stimulus to project work. As with field trips, this does not necessarily imply that the project begins with the visitor, although it can. One class of six-year-olds began a very interesting project on the circus after a "surprise" visit by a clown. More often, though, children will be prepared for the visitor, ready to focus in on what he or she has to say or with sets of questions to ask. Again the possibilities are endless. A brief list is given below of some popular project titles, with related people who may be persuaded to visit the class. Often these will be ordinary people who simply come to talk about their jobs. Of course, if these visitors can bring with them various objects of interest for the children to inspect or use, then so much the better.

People who help us. An obvious one to start. Visitors could include a police officer, fire fighter, nurse, delivery truck driver, postal worker, etc. Often these can be found among parents or relatives of children in the class.

Transportation. Human interest can be added to what sometimes become very mechanical projects by visits from an engine or bus driver, a station superintendent, a sailor (professional or amateur), a pilot, a flight attendant, etc.

Communications. One class began a successful project on films with a visit from a professional cartoonist. Other possibilities include a telephone operator, a postal worker, a photographer, a journalist, or a CB radio enthusiast.

Homes and houses. One class of six-year-olds doing a project on homes and houses was lucky enough to have a student whose father ran his own building business. He came and gave a demonstration of bricklaying, after which all the children had a turn. I think the wall is still standing! Other possibilities might include a real estate agent, a beekeeper (bees have homes, too), or a police officer to talk about house security.

Dinosaurs. A project like this might best begin with a trip to a museum with dinosaur remains, but if this is impossible the museum curator might visit and bring some fossils, photos, and slides with her. Sometimes amateur geology enthusiasts can be found who also have fossil collections.

Music. Obviously a visit by a musician or a group will start this project off well, but it might also be possible to get a musical instrument maker.

TELEVISION AND VIDEO

Many excellent projects have their origins in television programs the class watches together, and there can be no doubt that TV has a great deal of potential for stimulating children to do interesting work. It can show them things they could never see at first hand, and working with it has the useful spin-off that it may encourage them to watch more actively when they are at home. In fact, some of the material available is so good it is a shame that it gets watched only once. A videorecorder is almost an essential item of equipment to get the best use from TV programs. On video a program can be watched more than once, it can be stopped for discussion at any point, and groups of children can go back to sections they need to view again.

Traditional film tends not to be used much in schools now, having been almost entirely replaced by videotape. The flexibility of the latter makes this a very desirable development, and we must hope that all the excellent material previously available on film will eventually be transferred to video.

STORIES AND POETRY

Stories and poetry are an often-neglected starting point for project work but are, in fact, particularly useful because they act directly on children's imaginations. Longer stories or novels can be read in serialized form over several days or weeks. After each installment, the students can be engaged in following up themes or aspects of setting. They can also be invited to speculate on subsequent events.

Short stories can either be used independently or collected together. A project on animals, for instance, could include the sharing of several linked or stand-alone short stories involving different animals. A similar approach can be used with poems.

An interesting display of objects, pictures, books, and stories will always be a useful accompaniment to any of the above techniques for starting a project. It may also be a good starting point in its own right. In this case it is probably best to set up the display and give the children a few days to look at, handle, and ask about it before attempting to introduce the project. Interested children may wish to contribute to the display with objects of their own, and this is an excellent way of building up commitment.

Choosing and Developing Ideas

Almost all teachers, when starting a project with their students, will have some idea of the kinds of areas they hope to cover, even if these change and develop as the project proceeds. There are several useful techniques available to help in planning these areas. As the next section will discuss in more detail, it is important that the children be involved in this planning to as great an extent as possible. This section, however, concentrates on the teacher.

BEGINNING TO STRUCTURE PLANS

Most planning will begin in a fairly loose way, with the teacher (as much as possible in conjunction with the children) simply jotting down possible ideas for development as they come to mind. The important thing at this brainstorming stage is not to evaluate too much the ideas that occur, or to bother to think them through. That can be done later. The point at first is to collect ideas, and follow the flow as one idea leads to another. One teacher who regularly does this brainstorming with her class tells them that "ideas are like butterflies. If you don't catch them as they fly past, they quickly escape forever."

Having amassed a series of ideas for project activities, the teacher can then go through the list, marking those that now seem impractical or unlikely. It is best not to get rid of these entirely yet, as you never know how things might develop. What initially seems impossible might later be usable, perhaps in a modified form.

At some stage the teacher will need to sort out the gathered ideas into the curriculum areas they cover. This is done so that the teacher is aware of how the project will contribute to curriculum balance. Often doing this is sufficient to stimulate further ideas in curriculum areas that seem under-represented. It should not be thought, however, that every project must cover all the major areas. This is probably impossible, and to attempt it is likely to lead to a great deal of artificiality. There are some projects that simply do not lend themselves to certain areas of the curriculum; on the other hand, there are some curriculum areas—for instance, language and creative arts—which seem to find a central place in every project. As discussed in the previous chapter, the teacher does need to be aware of the areas the project is covering, though, for two main reasons:

— to check the areas in which extra work may need to be undertaken during the course of the project, so that these areas do not suffer unduly;
— to try to ensure a balance in the type of projects undertaken during the course of a year, with, say, an environmental studies project following a more mathematical one.

At this point teachers will need to think about scheduling project work. It is quite common for only one or two afternoons a week to be devoted to projects. Here the message is clearly that projects are an extra in the curriculum and do not have too much importance. But project work has much more potential than this. For it to be taken more seriously it needs more time, and certainly time of higher status—that is, mornings as well as afternoons. There are classrooms in which the entire week is spent on project work, and all curriculum areas are integrated into the project. This is probably too extreme for most teachers. Less extreme is the integrated approach, in which at most times, some children (but not the whole class) are working on their project. This allows the teacher to work with small groups and individuals as needed.

There is no single ideal way of giving time to project work. Sometimes it may be appropriate to devote an entire week to a project, and then not do any more for a month afterward. At other times, a regular day, or day and a half, may be better. Teachers should, of course, decide for themselves, bearing in mind the nature of the project, the needs of the children, and the importance placed on project work in the classroom and school.

The topic web is a very useful project-planning tool. It is a convenient way of organizing linked ideas together. It may be designed simply to show how one idea links to another or, more formally, it might include curriculum areas from which appropriate ideas stem. An example of each type is given in the figure.

FURTHER CONSIDERATIONS

The topic web is a useful format for generating ideas, but it does not really go far enough in the planning process as it ignores many areas that need to be considered. Attention needs to be given to what the end products of the project are going to be, what resources will be needed, how the classroom will be organized, and what deliberate teaching might be needed. The following checklist details the further planning that will be needed for the project.

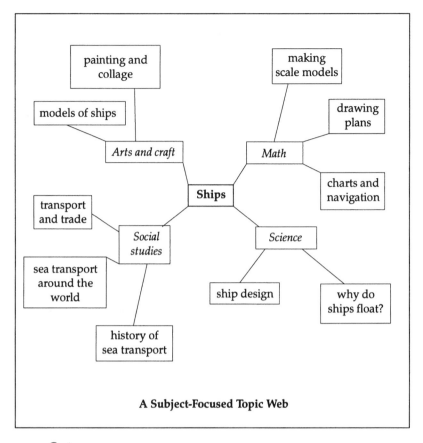

A Subject-Focused Topic Web

— *Outcome*

What will be produced by the end of the project? What forms will this take (books, wall charts, videos, tape-slide sets, etc.)? Who are the intended readers or users of the outcomes (children in the same or different classes, younger children, other schools, local community, etc.)?

— *Resources*

What kind of resources will be needed during the project? Where will these be obtained?

— *Organization*

How much time will be given to the project and how will it be scheduled? What areas of the classroom will be used for the project, either for working or display (project corner, topic table, etc.)? How will the class be grouped for project work? What use will be made of whole class, group, or individual work? Will project work be integrated into other curriculum areas, and, if so, how?

— *Intervention*
At what points in the project might it be profitable for the teacher to intervene with direct (skills or content) teaching?
— *Evaluation*
When and how might the teacher evaluate skill and concept development? What opportunities might there be for children to evaluate their own or their peers' work? How might outside evaluations be brought into the project?
— *Keeping track*
What records will be kept of individual, group, or class progress?

More detailed discussion of most of these issues is found later in the book. Planning in many of these areas should involve the children, but teachers need to be aware of them right from the outset of the planning process.

DEVELOPING LISTS OF GOALS

However long the planning process, it should end up with a very clear list of things the children will do in groups or as individuals during the project. As discussed in the next main section, drawing up this list should involve the children, and, if possible, they should be provided with a copy of the list on which tasks they are responsible for are clearly indicated. They can then check off the tasks as they complete them.

KEEPING FLEXIBILITY

As pointed out earlier, it would not be a good thing if planning at the beginning of the project turned into a very rigid process, after which nothing was allowed to be changed. Planning must be kept flexible, and allowance must be made for changes as the project proceeds. These changes might come about because

— children get extremely involved in one aspect and wish to do more detailed work on it,
— an unexpected event occurs which provides an opportunity for a change in emphasis, or
— children lose interest in one aspect, or their enthusiasm does not last as long as expected.

If negotiation is taken seriously as a process, then planning will never really stop. The teacher and the children can be discussing what is happening all the time, and changes, minor or major, can be made with the agreement of everyone.

Involving the Children

Readers will already have little doubt that I am a great proponent of involving children in project planning. This is not only a way of ensuring their enthusiasm for and commitment to the project (although it should certainly help with that), but it also functions importantly as a learning experience. As noted previously, children will not always have a teacher on hand to plan their activities for them. They must, at some stage, learn to do this themselves. Involving them as much as possible in the planning of projects can develop the independence that they need to acquire. This section will discuss strategies for doing this.

NEGOTIATION

Obviously young children are not going to be in a position immediately to plan a project on their own. Nobody would recommend simply letting them take over without providing appropriate guidance. This would likely lead only to superficiality at best and, at worst, to chaos. Project planning is an important opportunity for teaching, and the teacher needs to give a lot of time to guiding, encouraging, and, occasionally, directing the children. Perhaps the best way of doing this is through negotiation, which simply means working alongside the children in their decision-making processes. At each stage of a project, the teacher should discuss with the children what is going to happen, listen to their ideas, contribute his or her own, and work with them to come to joint decisions. This kind of process can concern as many of the details of the project as the teacher can bear. Questions such as the following might be discussed:

— What activities will be included in our project?
— How will these activities be organized?
— What forms of grouping will be used?
— Who will be responsible for what?
— What resources will be needed?
— Where will these be obtained?
— Who will get them?
— How will they be stored?

— How will the furniture be arranged?
— How will the display space be arranged?
— How much time will be devoted to the project?
— How will this time be used?
— How will everyone know where they are in their work on the project?

These decisions have to be made by somebody in the classroom, and, of course, this is usually the teacher. Involving the children in these decisions, to whatever extent is feasible, is a good way of developing their ability to think and act independently. This can be begun at a very early stage in school. There are naturally limits to what children are capable of doing at various ages, but one thing is completely certain: If they are never given the chance to try, and sometimes to make a complete mess of the whole thing, they will never become capable.

STRATEGIES

A very useful strategy at the beginning of a project is brainstorming. This involves the children in a purposeful and entertaining way, although it can be hard work for the teacher, who has the responsibility of writing everything down. (Some older children might just be able to manage this for themselves, but most younger children will find it too difficult; one needs to be able to write very quickly but still legibly.) Brainstorming involves everybody in the class or group contributing ideas as quickly as they can, with little attempt at first to evaluate their feasibility or suitability; this will come later. The ideas are written down by the appointed scribe as they are called out. It is probably easiest to use an overhead projector for this, as this allows ease of writing as well as permitting the teacher to face the group. The teacher will also be contributing ideas, so it is clear that the task, although very worthwhile, is not an easy one.

When sufficient ideas have been gathered (or the teacher is exhausted!), they have then to be structured in some way. If the session is concerned with ideas for what will be done in the project, then structuring will involve grouping ideas together according to similar features. Grouping into curriculum areas, as described in the previous section, will probably not mean much to the children and is really a way for the teacher to ensure curriculum balance. With children, grouping should focus on dividing the project up into topic areas.

Let's look at the process in action at the beginning of a class project on cars. This class of nine- and ten-year-olds watched an educational TV program about the development of the car and brainstormed afterward about questions they could research in their project. This resulted in a list of eighteen ideas. The next step

History and Development	Types	Roads
old cars	racing cars	motorways
the first car	Rolls-Royces	roads
wheels	kinds of cars	
car design	cars around the world*	
How Cars Work	Learning to Drive	Uses
car engines	highway code*	motor racing
how a car works	learning to drive*	trucks
		buses
		ambulances

was to sort the ideas into topics. Together the class and the teacher rearranged the list under the headings shown in the figure. (Items marked with an asterisk were contributed by the teacher.) It quickly became clear that some of the ideas were quite broad and could serve as headings in their own right ("learning to drive," for example) while others were more specific.

The children then organized themselves, with some guidance and suggestions from the teacher, into six groups, each of which would concentrate on one of the topics. The groups then spent some time on further brainstorming and idea structuring with their own subtopics. The teacher arranged class activities so that only one group at a time was working on this, so she was able to be with each group. This allowed her to add her own ideas to the children's and to ensure that what they planned was feasible. At the end of this process, each group had a list of things they hoped to do and had allocated responsibility for particular tasks to group members.

This process took over a week. During this time group members were beginning to read about their topics and collect resources from various places, which gave them fresh ideas. Although this seems a long time to devote to planning with little having been produced as yet, much had actually been achieved. The children in each group had

— discussed their topic in general terms,
— familiarized themselves with the areas to be covered,
— gained a clear idea of what they were aiming to achieve,
— taken on clear individual responsibilities within the group's work,
— worked out a rough time schedule for their work,
— planned their program with the teacher to ensure that they would cover skills she felt them capable of and ready for.

GIVING RESPONSIBILITY

Children learn to be independent by being given responsibility for their own actions and facing the consequences if things go wrong. This inevitably means that they will make a great many mistakes, but as long as these are treated as experiences to be learned from, they can be positive. Of course, being given responsibility does not mean being left to flounder. Children are learners and they do need the guidance of their teacher—as long as this allows them scope to make and live with decisions.

Examples of this approach range from the tiny to the grand. A tiny example concerns a group of eight-year-olds who were working on the history of flight for a class project on flight. The usual pattern in the classroom was for the teacher to plan and mount wall displays of the children's work as it progressed. The students in this group asked if, this time, they could be given one of the display spaces and allowed to plan and mount their own work. The teacher agreed somewhat hesitantly, expecting that her usual high standard of display would be let down. The end product, while not perfect by any means, was, however, considerably better than she had expected. Thinking back, she realized why. The children knew they lacked their teacher's expertise in display, and at several points they had come to her to ask for advice (although they had not always accepted it). They had decided she was a consultant, and had used her as such.

The grander example concerns a class of six-year-olds who

made a trip to a farm as part of a project on animals. Children in the class made all the arrangements for the trip, from contacting the farm about their proposed visit and its purpose to booking a bus and working out the cost per child. Of course, the teacher had made all these arrangements beforehand, and warned the various people to expect telephone calls and letters from the children. But the children did not know this, and they believed that the responsibility for arranging the visit properly was entirely theirs. They took this responsibility very seriously indeed.

Choosing Resources and Planning Access

While planning the project, attention needs to be given to the resources that will be used and to how these might be made available to the children. The range of possible resources is discussed in a later chapter; at this point I want to concentrate primarily on print materials that will be kept within the school and to consider the question of access.

ENSURING BREADTH

Teachers should plan to include as full a range of resources as possible. Consider giving children the experience of using

— books
— magazines
— brochures
— advertisements
— pamphlets
— forms
— timetables
— instructions
— encyclopedias
— questionnaires
— maps
— dictionaries
— computer databases
— slide sets
— audiorecordings
— videorecordings
— stories
— poems

— posters

— and, the most important resource of all, people.

In the case of some resources, such as books from the school library, it will be possible only to keep a central stock. If these are borrowed and kept in the classroom for the duration of the project, this is likely to deprive the rest of the school. But keeping resources centrally creates an immediate problem of access. Children will need to borrow items from the central collection with some regularity, which means

1. the collection has to be organized so they can find what they need without wasting too much time,
2. they have to be taught how to find items in the collection,
3. they have to be able to replace borrowed items in the correct place,
4. they have to be able to use the collection without being under the direct supervision of the teacher.

If any of these conditions cannot be met, it does not mean the children cannot use the central collection but simply that it is going to require more assistance from the teacher. Once or twice a week during the project, you will probably need to take the class or a group to the collection to help students get the resources they need. This, of course, can be a good time for teaching them to use the collection, so it may serve a valuable additional purpose.

For all their difficulties, centralized resource collections in schools are worth maintaining for a number of reasons. They do permit a wider and more varied collection of resources than would be practical for a classroom library. Using a school library is also good practice for using the public library. Teachers are generally motivated to teach their students to use school collections properly, since everybody soon complains when resources get messy and disorganized.

ACCESS: CLASS COLLECTIONS

It is desirable, even if the bulk of print materials is kept in a central school library, for the class to have its own collection of heavily used resources. This simplifies things considerably and, for young children, might be the only really feasible way of ensuring the books are used sensibly and well. Use of class collections can be easily supervised by the teacher, and bad habits more easily prevented from developing in the children.

The need for class resource collections to be well organized is not often considered. Because such collections are usually fairly small, perhaps only thirty books or so, it is usually easy for children to find what they want just by browsing. This is, however, building up a very bad strategy for searching for information. This, in fact, ends up being how many children will go about looking for a book in a large library and is obviously extremely inefficient. Why not use the simplicity of a small book collection to begin to teach good habits from the beginning? To do this you should ensure that the collection, however small, is organized in some clear way. This may be by alphabetical order of authors' names, or, perhaps more usefully, by subject area. If each book is given an identifying number or color, and the key to these is displayed near the collection, children can be repeatedly encouraged to use the system to speed up their search for a book. When they visit a larger library, they will at least be familiar with the principle of library classification.

It may be that a special collection of books has been obtained for use in a project, perhaps from the district library service. In this case, the classification system can be reinforced if the children help in sorting and organizing the collection.

RESOURCES FROM OUTSIDE SCHOOL

Many projects will benefit from outside resources. This can add a more adult, realistic flavor to the project, and can also develop children's independence in acquiring sources of information. Examples include holiday brochures, telephone directories, advertising leaflets, application forms of various kinds, instruction leaflets, notices, magazines, and timetables. These and other similar items can be used in a variety of projects. But if the teacher simply collects and brings them into class, then a valuable opportunity is missed. Why not ask the children to collect them themselves? If this is discussed beforehand and children delegated to acquire particular materials, then a great deal of learning about information in the adult world is being done. As an example of this, in a project on vacations, children collected the following items:

- A group of six persuaded their parents to take them to various travel agents to acquire vacation brochures.
- Two children borrowed their parents' passports so that the rest of the class could use them as models to make their own.
- All the children acquired passport applications from local post offices.
- Half the class brought in out-of-date Yellow Pages.
- Most of the class wrote to various tourist boards for information.
- Several children visited the local railway station information office and brought back timetables, publicity materials, etc.

Planning the Physical Context

When embarking on a project there are several decisions concerning the classroom itself that need consideration. How should the furniture be arranged? How should resources be arranged and displayed? How should the work resulting from the project be displayed? As discussed earlier, there is much to be gained from making these decisions in cooperation with the children.

ARRANGING THE CLASSROOM

Few elementary classrooms today have the furniture permanently arranged so that all the children sit in rows facing the front of the class. This can be a very effective way of arranging things if the lesson involves the teacher presenting material to the whole class, such as when showing a video. It will be less effective, however, when the children are discussing and producing their work together. For this, the familiar groups of tables are more appropriate.

When children are working on a project, they might end up with several books and other resources in front of them, as well as their notebooks and project folders. This can lead to considerable crowding of the usual amount of work space. It will be a great help if children can "spill over" into other areas to create more room. If it is possible, a few extra tables set up somewhere in the classroom—say, as a project corner—will accommodate this. Some children may be quite happy working on the floor.

Another consideration concerns how children might work

together on large items, such as wall charts or friezes. This demands large spaces on which the work can be spread out. One possibility is to use a corridor or hall but, if this is not possible, some further rearrangement of classroom furniture will be necessary.

All these points lead toward the conclusion that the teacher will have to accept a much more flexible physical arrangement than the "one child, one desk" system. Arrangements may even need to change from lesson to lesson. Flexibility in this will, of course, require greater organizational skills from the teacher, and also greater awareness of everything going on in the classroom. In addition, children should be prepared and trained to help with rearrangements without fuss, so that time will not be wasted.

SPACE FOR DISPLAY

Most projects will generate a lot of work that can be displayed for others to see. Indeed, the display will often be what the project is working toward. Finding space for display, unless you happen to have a classroom with walls conveniently made of nicely colored bulletin boards, can be a problem. This is something that needs attention while the project is being planned so that children are not disheartened by producing work which cannot be displayed for lack of space. Here are some points for consideration:

— There is little point displaying children's written work above their eye level. If other children cannot read it, it is wasted.

— If space on the walls is at a premium, consider extending it by using rolls of corrugated cardboard, three-dimensional displays with writing on stand-up labels or zig-zag books, mobiles made from plastic hoops from which writing and pictures can be hung, or large signs suspended from the ceiling on which writing can be hung.

— Three-dimensional displays using tables draped with cloth always look effective.

Finally, keep in mind that displays are not art galleries where you stand in front of finished works and admire. Rather, they are developing collections that reflect the work children are doing, and stimulate further work.

As mentioned earlier, resources that are kept in the classroom for the duration of the project require arranging in some logical order. Some of them will probably form part of an initial display around the project, while others can be classified and sorted on a shelf or two. Think about displaying them in two or more areas of the classroom if possible, since this will cut down on the crush that is likely to develop as all the children try to find books at once. Clear labels will help children know exactly where to go and where to return books when they have finished with them. Children can be appointed as resource monitors, with the job of ensuring that everything is put back tidily in the correct place at the end of each session.

Planning the Social Context

In addition to the physical organization of the classroom, attention needs to be given to the social organization. How to organize groups of children is foremost among the questions here, but teachers also need to consider how to use each child's particular talents to the best effect while still ensuring all-round development.

GROUPING

Organizing children into groups for project work is a very popular strategy and can give a great deal of flexibility. It means that the whole class need not be involved in the same task simultaneously, and is consequently economical of resources and teacher time. Group work also provides the potential for a great deal of learning through discussion. It is well to notice, however, that much group work tends not to engender the discussion it might because the children in the group simply get on with their individual task rather than cooperating. This is largely the fault of the kinds of tasks they are doing. If the teacher wants to encourage learning through discussion, then the tasks children do must require discussion—that is, they must be joint tasks. If group members have to cooperate to produce a single end product, they have to discuss as they go along.

The size of the group will influence the benefits children get from working this way. Obviously it must not be too big, or they will not all get the chance to contribute. Six is probably a maximum size, unless the task they are doing is very big. Neither must the group be too small, as this places too much responsibility for generating ideas on too few children. Three is a minimum desirable number.

The composition of the group needs consideration. For some tasks a group of children of similar ability might be better; for others, a mixed ability group might get the best out of all its members. The key point is to be flexible and to see grouping as related to specific activities, rather than hard and fast for always.

USING PARTICULAR TALENTS

Children with special talents can come into their own in project work, when they not only contribute their specialty to the work of their group but may also act as consultants to the rest of the class. The obvious example of this is a child with special artistic talents, but there are children with other talents, such as knowledge about computers or railway trains, or with musical abilities that can be used by the whole class. These children's image of themselves can improve immensely as a result of being cast in a special role.

Remember, though, that just because children have special talents they do not have to spend all their time using them. This is bad policy for two reasons. First, it limits these children's chances to develop other equally important abilities. Second, it can deprive other children in the class of the opportunity to practice and learn skills that come easily to these children. For this reason, the "consultancy" approach should be favored over the "specialist" approach. Rather than insisting that children follow a resident specialist's instructions, they can be given the opportunity to ask a consultant if they choose. In this way both the "consultors" and the "consultees" can benefit by sharing knowledge in a relaxed social context.

In this chapter I have examined some of the issues to be taken into consideration when planning a project in your classroom. I want to conclude by reiterating the desirability of involving the students in this planning as much as possible. There is immense learning potential in such involvement.

. . . .

PLANNING PROJECT

OUTCOMES

In the previous chapter I suggested that children need to begin a project with a clear set of ideas about what they are aiming to achieve by its completion. In other words, they should know

— what end products will arise from the project (booklets, wall charts, three-dimensional models, presentations, etc.)
— the audiences for these end products (classmates, other children in the school, younger children, adults in the community, and so on).

This does not mean that plans for end products should be completely inflexible once they have been decided. As the project progresses new ideas may emerge and the original ones may well be changed or expanded. Neither does this suggest that end products should be the sole emphasis of the project. Indeed, from the teacher's point of view, what is produced at the end is, in a way, of quite minor importance. In terms of the learning that project work can engender, the process the children go through is far more important than what they actually produce.

Two examples, which many teachers will recognize, make this clear. In the first, a group of children have produced a beautifully presented booklet about ships. It has a table of contents, from which it can be seen that each page is concerned with a different type of ship. On each page there is a cut-out color illustration of a particular ship and underneath two or three paragraphs of very neat writing about it. On closer inspection, it is obvious that almost all the writing has been painstakingly copied from reference books. Another group, however, has produced a rather ragged poster about airplanes. In the center is a hand-drawn picture of a jumbo jet, with labels attached to its various parts. Under this is a description of one child's journey in such a plane. Around the edges are sketches of other types of airplanes, accompanied by pieces of writing ranging from poems to imaginary accounts of flying. All the writing has spelling mistakes and crossings out, and some of it is written in a style which is quite hard to read.

It is likely that both groups had a similar outcome in mind when they began their work and in terms of attention to their product, the first group seems to have come out best. But what have they actually learned in the process of producing their booklet? Their learning may be limited to further confirmation in their minds that the end product is of paramount importance in project work. The children in the second group certainly need some assistance with the presentation of their work, but they have undoubtedly learned far more, both by looking carefully at pictures and by trying to link information they have found to their own experiences.

This is not to imply, of course, that the product is of no importance. In the adult world we are often judged according to what we produce. The end product of any task we undertake is usually the only visible result of our efforts, and it should be adequate for its purpose. Children need to learn how to make what they produce adequate for the situation and appropriate for the people who will receive it. In addition, we must accept that the product is usually the thing children are aiming for in a project. Most children are very aware when their products are lacking in some way, and no amount of reassuring them that they have learned a lot in the process will help.

Attention must, therefore, be given to the end products of project work, although the importance of the process should never be forgotten. In this chapter I discuss some of the ways in which children might present their work. But first I look at the important idea of audience, and suggest possible audiences for project outcomes.

Aiming for an Audience

When adults communicate, whether orally or through writing or other media, they usually have a fairly clear idea of the audience that will receive their communication. Awareness of this audience can obviously have a very marked effect on the format and content of that communication. If I am involved in a car crash, I may write about the events in a letter to my insurance company and also in a letter to my best friend. The basic information I am communicating will be the same in both cases, but, of course, the particular details I include and the style in which I write will be very different. It would not be appropriate to write in the same way to both audiences.

Most adults are aware of the influence of audience and act accordingly. They become aware of it through a great deal of experience in using language for a range of purposes and in a variety of settings—that is, by sending and receiving communications. Young children, who haven't had the benefit of such wide-ranging experience of language use, will not be sufficiently aware unless they are shown. Fortunately, it is possible to provide a range of audiences for school children, and project work lends itself especially to this. Some possible audiences are discussed in what follows.

THE TEACHER

Even if completed project work is destined eventually for another audience, the first people to look at it will almost always be teachers. Therefore, their reactions to this work are crucial. There are a number of ways in which teachers can receive children's work and thereby provide different categories of audience.

The teacher as a trusted adult. Usually teachers want children to regard them as people who can be trusted to view their work sympathetically and help them with it. Teachers who manage to get their students to think of them in this way are in privileged positions. Not only is mutual trust a very sound basis for effective learning and teaching, but it can also provide specific opportunities for children to develop their abilities, particularly in their writing. One of the best ways for children to learn about writing is for them to experiment—that is to try out new words, expressions, techniques, and genres. To encourage them to do this, teachers must react positively to such experiments. To respond simply by criticizing or by marking experiments as mistakes will destroy children's trust in the audience of their teacher and discourage them from trying new things in future.

The teacher as an examiner. When teachers receive children's work it is very often in their role as examiners. The language used to describe the process indicates this clearly. Teachers "mark" or "grade" children's work; they "correct" mistakes. This can, rather too often, have the effect described above of discouraging children rather than encouraging them. This is the familiar negative side of the examiner audience that the teacher provides.

There can be, however, a more positive side to the teacher's examiner role. Most children, when they are producing work they think is important—especially if it is going to be read by people outside their classroom—are very keen that the work be presentable and correct. Most children are capable of taking pride in their work when given the opportunity and encouragement to produce their best. Teachers are invaluable in this process since they can judge children's work with more experienced eyes than those of the children themselves. Children can use their teachers as preliminary testers of their work before passing it on to its intended audience. Thus, teachers' abilities to examine are very useful.

It should be noted that for the teacher to assume this examiner role successfully, the children must recognize that there is a task to be done and their teacher is the best equipped person to help them with it. It is a very positive sign indeed if children approach teachers with their work, asking for it to be corrected. This means they have both recognized the need to present their work in its best light and decided that the teacher is the best person to comment on whether this has been done.

The teacher in a special role. With some creative thinking, teachers can provide audiences that are geared to particular projects. For example, in one project, a class of ten- and eleven-year-olds made plans for how best to use a vacant lot near their school. One group pretended they were property developers, and put forward their plans accordingly. A second group pretended to be local farmers, and a third, an environmental pressure group. Part of the project involved the children writing letters to argue their case to people such as government officials and local residents. These letters were actually sent to their teacher, who replied to each in the correct role.

In another project some seven- and eight-year-olds, after reading Ted Hughes's *The Iron Man*, designed new homes for an Iron Man. Their designs were sent to the teacher, who replied to each in the role of an Iron Man, with an assessment of how appropriate the design would be for him.

In a project on magic, six- and seven-year-olds wrote magic spells and sent them to a witch to test out. The witch (the teacher) wrote back to each child with an account of what happened when he tried the spells. This turned into a longer running project than the teacher had anticipated, as some children wrote back with suggested improvements to their spells. They eventually picked out the best spells and sent them to the witch in a bound, presentation volume. He, of course, replied with a lovely thank you letter.

In none of these examples did the children actually believe that the people they wrote to were real. They were able to suspend disbelief, however, because of the teachers' abilities to carry off their roles successfully and play the appropriate audience.

OTHER CHILDREN

Beyond the teacher, an obvious audience for children's project work is that provided by other children. There are many ways in which this audience might be used. The suggestions following are only starting points.

Children in the same class. Producing project work to be read by classmates is something most children do at some stage. This usually occurs when the children finish pieces of work which are then displayed in the classroom in such a way that other children can look at and read them. The audience here is almost incidental. To develop children's sensitivity to the needs of various audiences, this sort of display really needs to be extended so that children deliberately produce work with their classmates in mind. There are several ways this can be done. For example, children can be given time to present their work to the rest of the class. This will probably happen as children complete their projects, but presentation of work in progress can occur at regular intervals. As will be discussed later, this sort of ongoing presentation can be a useful strategy in teachers' evaluation of the children's learning. Furthermore, it reminds children to keep audience in mind as they pursue their project. Of course, the teacher will need to be prepared to give advice on presentation styles and techniques as the children require it.

When a project is intended to result in some kind of whole-class presentation of work—such as a class book, magazine, or central display—a group of children can be given the role of editorial board. All work produced will go to this board (perhaps via the teacher), whose role is to advise on its suitability, perhaps suggest changes, and select pieces for the final product. This approach results in two audiences: whoever will see the final class product, and the editorial board that approves material for this final product. This has the effect of sharpening considerably the appreciation of audience in all the children, but especially in those on the board. These children have to judge the appropriateness for the intended audience of work given to them, justify to others why they feel particular pieces are not appropriate as they stand, and give useful guidance on how work might be presented more appropriately. Naturally, composition of this board can be varied so that most children get the chance to be members at some stage.

Another approach is to have children present their project work in forms that can be stored permanently in the classroom library, and thus be read and used by other children in the class. This is a particularly valuable activity as it not only encourages children to consider their audience but also gives their work a very high status. Project end products intended for the class library will need to be bound, with appropriate information about authorship prominently displayed.

Children in other classes. The two fairly common ways that project work is shared with other classes are by wall displays in a common area of the school (for example, a corridor or assembly hall) or presentations delivered at a whole-school meeting. The latter can be particularly useful, as it requires children to tailor their material to the wide range of ages and abilities they will find in front of them.

These two techniques are, however, inevitably limited in their effects on children's audience awareness because of the limited opportunity they offer for real feedback. Children will only learn about the needs of an audience if they have the opportunity to find out the responses of that audience to their work. Other techniques do allow for this feedback. For example, classes can pair up to work on linked projects. In one case of this, a class of nine- and ten-year-olds and another of eight- to ten-year-olds decided to do a project together on the development of land transport, focusing specially on their home area. One class decided to specialize in rail transport and the other in roads. The classes were occasionally brought together to view transparencies and videos about transportation, and they knew they were working toward a joint display. A feature of the project was the swapping of completed pieces of work. Both classes found that regularly gaining information about topics related to their own gave them fresh insights into their areas and caused them to rethink their own work. This technique is really only suitable, however, when students in the two classes are of roughly equal maturity and ability.

In another approach, older students can produce project work for younger ones. This clearly has benefits for the older children since it gives their work a real purpose and audience, but it can also benefit the younger ones since the end product could be "information books" specifically designed for them, to supplement their class libraries. In an example of this, one class of eight- and nine-year-olds did a project on animals, part of which involved their preparing booklets on wild animals for a six- and seven-year-old class. They began by borrowing examples of the information books that were already in the younger class, which they then studied to assess their format and style of writing. (Another approach to this would be for the older students to visit the younger ones to talk about the kind of books they use.) The children then decided that they would produce twelve short booklets, each dealing with one animal. They discussed the issue of format and decided that, given the age of their audience, they needed lots of pictures and only small amounts of writing. Each of the six project groups in the older class took responsibility for two booklets. When the books were finished but not yet bound, one representative from each group took their books to the younger class and let some of the children there read and talk about them. As a result of this consumer research, the representatives were able to suggest some changes to the booklets to their groups. These were made, and the books were bound in hard covers. They were then presented to the audience class and became a proud addition to their class library.

In addition to producing project books for class libraries, children can also contribute to the stock of the school library, where they can form an extremely useful extra resource. They can be stored as a special collection or completely integrated into the rest of the library, with their own Dewey numbers. Remember, though, that for this use books will certainly need to use good quality paper and be securely bound.

Children in other schools. Producing project work for children in other schools can provide a real purpose for the presentation of this work and help develop an awareness of audience. There are many ways in which this can be done. Two examples illustrate the possibilities. In one, a class of nine- and ten-year-old children established a relationship with a similar class in a different part of the country. Their teachers had been friends at college. The two classes were paired one for one and students regularly kept in touch with each other as pen pals, but they also exchanged project work. At the beginning of the year each class began with a project on their local environment. The explicit purpose for this was to tell their new friends all about where they lived. As one school was situated in a rural area in the north of England and the other in a London suburb, there were many differences to learn about. The classes exchanged project booklets, photographs, and audiotapes, and each mounted a display in their classroom about the other's area.

In another part of the country, two classes of seven- and eight-year-olds from different parts of a large city each began the school year with a project entitled "Ourselves." Copies of completed work were swapped between the classes and again used in displays by the receiving class. Audio- and videotapes were also exchanged, and the project worked toward a joint party at which students from both classes could meet one another.

A third possibility for this kind of work is to set up correspondence with children in other countries. Often a town-twinning association will be able to help arrange this.

OTHER ADULTS

Producing work for adults besides the teacher is within the capabilities of most students and can have a great impact in making their project work "real" to them. There are several possibilities.

Parents. Parents are the obvious audience to consider first. Many parents only get to look at their children's work on parents' night. Generally this work is not prepared specially for them, so its creation doesn't contribute to development of children's audience awareness. Parents can, though, be targeted as the chief audience for particular pieces of project work. Projects about the school, the local environment, or the children themselves are perhaps most appropriate for this. Parents who volunteer at the school or are able to come in occasionally can also be brought into a project to serve as an extra audience to the teacher. They will need to be given careful guidance on how to respond to children's work, but there is no reason why they cannot fulfill any of the audience roles specified earlier for the teacher.

Visitors and other project helpers. If a project has involved a visitor of some kind, the children can produce work to send to this visitor. Most people who visit schools to talk to the children would be extremely pleased to receive work done as a result of their visit.

The same applies to other people who may have assisted with the project. For example, the local postmaster may have written back to children with answers to questions, as might the local railway station manager, etc. Local people may have been inter-viewed by children—for example, the manager of the supermarket or a community police officer. Sending these people copies of work produced as a result of their efforts will not only give the children practice in preparing material for a real audi-ence, but will also make it more likely that these people will take the trouble to help other children and schools in the future.

Local newspapers. Local newspapers are often very pleased to feature work done by schools. Often they will report the work rather than print it in the form in which the children produced it. Regardless, the children will first of all need to create their materi-als in a way that will make the newspaper notice them and want to include the work in some way. Many newspapers have News-paper in Education coordinators attached to them, whose role it is to make links between newspapers and schools. They will proba-bly be delighted to receive examples of children's project work and can often be persuaded to commission children to write about particular topics.

End Products

What commonly seems to happen in projects is that a fairly lim-ited range of formats is actually used for the presentation of chil-dren's work. In fact, there are many possible ways in which children can present information they have found out during the course of their project work. In what follows I discuss some possi-bilities for physical presentation as well as some of the writing styles and other methods of communication that can be used.

Booklets. Perhaps the most popular form of presentation is the project booklet. Generally, each child in the class has his or her own small booklet in which work on the project is recorded in words or drawings. Sometimes these booklets are store-bought exercise books, and sometimes they are homemade books of folded paper inside a card cover. Making books like this can be a valuable part of the project.

Booklets like these do have their drawbacks. They can limit the nature of what children produce in project work: if it does not fit into the booklet, then it does not count. They also enforce a more or less linear approach to the work. It is very difficult for children to go back to work already in the booklet and revise or add to it since there will probably not be room.

Loose-leaf folders. Folders that allow pages to be taken out and new ones inserted are much more flexible than prebound booklets. They enable children to go back to a piece of work and revise or rewrite it. They also allow the work amassed on a project to be rearranged into different orders. Pages of several children's work on particular aspects of the project can be removed in order to make a class booklet, or individual pieces can be taken out for display.

The design of folders like this is important. Clearly the ideal is a folder or binder with metal rings that click open and shut, if the cost of one of these for every child can be afforded. If not, methods such as tying work together with wool or string can be used, though these are difficult for children to manage and are therefore never very satisfactory.

Posters and wall charts. Presenting project work on wall charts has some advantages over booklet presentation. Artwork and written material can easily be linked, with one informing the other. Artwork that is too bulky to fit in a booklet can also be included in a wall chart or poster.

Such displays can be designed in several ways. One begins with a simple version of the topic web that was used to plan the project and collects work around each of the web subtopics. For example, a wall chart on animals might have the title in the center and the subtitles "Farm Animals," "Pets," "Wild Animals," and "Working Animals" in each corner. Paintings, drawings, writing, and charts could then be displayed around each subtitle.

Another design is built around a large illustration. For example, a wall chart about airports might consist of a large frieze of an airport, with a plane on the runway, the airport buildings, and some of the workers. Beside each feature might be a piece of writing about it, either on the illustration itself or at the edge with a length of wool or a marker line joining feature and writing.

Other designs might be more specific. A chart on dinosaurs might include pictures of eight types of dinosaur drawn to scale, one beneath the other, with facts and figures about each written in beside. Alternatively the chart might be based on a time line, with defined periods accompanied by pictures and information about the dinosaurs common at those times.

The best approach obviously depends on the needs of the particular project, but in general, there is a great deal to be gained if children are involved in the design. They may see possibilities the teacher does not, and will certainly learn a great deal by working out measurements and so on.

Writing frames. Regardless of the form of display, most projects will involve a piece of writing as all or part of the end product. This writing is most often expository, a form that can be very difficult for children. One way to support children's attempts at expository writing structures during project work is to introduce them to writing frames. These consist of key words or phrases, constructed according to particular genres, around which children compose. For a sequential report, for example, children might be given this template:

First the mother frog _____

Then she _____

Next _____

Then _____

And finally_____

For comparison/contrast,

Insects and spiders are alike in several ways. They both have _____

_____

They also both_____

_____

However, they are also different. Insects _____

_____

while spiders_____

_____

Another difference between them is _____

_____

For reaction,

Although I already knew that _____

_____

when I was working on this project I learned that _____

_____

I also learned that_____

_____

and that _____

_____

Such templates of connectives and sentence modifiers give the children a structure within which they can concentrate on communicating what they want to say, rather than getting lost in how to say it. One group of nine-year-olds, for example, had collected pages of directly copied notes in their folders as part of a project entitled "Underground." The children were asked to talk about one thing they had found during their research that had made them think, "Oh, that's really interesting. I didn't know that," or any discovery that had made them change their minds about the subject. After a lively discussion the teacher introduced a writing frame and modeled on a previously prepared oversize copy how their information could be written up. The children were asked to select a frame to guide their own writing. The writing produced by one girl, shown in the illustration, indicates very clearly her personal interpretations of the information.

Fiction. An often-neglected way of presenting information is to use it as the basis for a piece of narrative. This can be especially useful in history, where dry historical facts can come alive if they form the background for a story. As an example of this, one group of eight-year-olds decided to tell the story of a Viking voyage. Before they could do this sensibly, they needed to find out about

— the design of Viking ships
— where the Vikings sailed
— why they made long voyages
— how they organized themselves
— the kinds of preparations they made
— what problems they might encounter.

These questions were used to guide their reading in books and encyclopedias. They gathered their information under each heading and used their findings to plan their story. This was written collaboratively, with each child taking responsibility for a section and then the whole group commenting and suggesting changes. This resulted in an excellent piece of narrative writing, with a very authentic background.

Pamphlets. By "pamphlet" I mean a very short booklet—say, four to six pages—dealing with one very specific topic. In any project, children might produce several pamphlets. For example, in a project on communications, eight-year-olds produced pamphlets on the telephone, television, radio, the postal service, and computers. Having to produce short, snappy pamphlets forces children to condense the information they accumulate on their topics and to pick out the essential items. Children can be given a very good model for this if they are shown some of the many pamphlets that various firms or institutions—for example, the post office—produce. Pamphlets provide an excellent way of getting children to think about the value of each word they use as they are writing.

Mary's Writing about Rabbits

Before I began this topic I thought that the male rabbits where the ones who dug the warrens. But when I red about it. I found out that it was actual the females who did all the work, as usual!

I also learnt that the passages or burrows are up to 3m long and 15 cm wide so the rabbits can get though easily.

Secondly I learnt that the warren can be over 30 years old and around 30 rabbits can live in one.

Finally I learnt that the rabbits warren has lots of ways in and out, so if one is blocked a rabbit can get in another.

Also a warren is only for one family.

Quizzes. Designing quizzes about a project area for other members of the class can be a real stimulus for children to accumulate information. Obviously before they can ask sensible questions in a quiz, they need not only to know the answers themselves but also to have a sufficiently broad understanding to decide what the important questions are.

Quizzes can be set simply, with the children counting their right answers, or more complicated competitions might be devised. Each project group could perhaps set a number of questions, which could then be displayed. The whole class would have two or three days to find as many answers as possible, either working individually or in their groups. Another competition might run along the lines of Trivial Pursuit, with each group responsible for a category.

Diagrams. It will very often be more appropriate for children to present information in diagrammatic form than in simple written prose. To prepare a diagram, children really have to understand the information they are presenting; in addition, such presentation is impossible simply to copy from books. There are many types of diagrams which they may use, depending on the type of information they are dealing with. The matrix example is the result of a project on animals in which eight and nine-year-olds

Diagramming Information

Type of animal / Characteristic	Mammal	Reptile	Insect	Bird	Fish
warm blooded	✔	✘	✘	✔	✘
lays eggs	*	✔	✔	✔	✔
has lungs	✔	✔	✘	✔	*
flies	*	✘	*	✔	✘
suckles young	✔	✘	✘	✘	✘
has skin	✔	✘	✘	✔	✘
has scales	✘	✔	✘	✘	✔
lives in water	*	*	*	*	✔

✔ = yes; ✘ = no; * = sometimes

discovered how animals might be classified. Other types of diagrams include graphs (e.g., a block graph to show which countries, states, or provinces children have visited on their vacations), maps (e.g., a map showing railway lines in a particular area), and flow charts (e.g., a flow chart showing the sequence of events in the production of electricity).

Audiorecordings. The products of project work do not, of course, have to be written. There are many benefits when children produce audiotapes about their project. They will still have to think carefully about presentation of the information, but in a different way. Since simply reading an account of what they have found into a tape recorder will be rather dull, children will need to think of alternatives. They may find that relating their material through stories or poems is more exciting. Mock interviews or documentary-style presentations may also be more engaging for the listener. Children might also consider using other media, with their taped commentary linked to the showing of slides or pictures. A single tape might include a mixture of these styles and formats. One of the chief benefits of this form of presentation is that it does not discriminate against children with poor handwriting.

Video. Most of the remarks about sound recordings apply also to videorecordings, although these have extra potential in that they allow the close linking of picture and sound. The use of video as a means of presenting project work is obviously limited to those schools with access to a videorecorder and camera. If the equipment is available, it does allow children to practice a whole range of new skills and encourages a great deal of attention to presentation and its impact. Those schools not fortunate enough to possess their own equipment may find that a local high school or college may lend these items, and even provide staff or students to show children how to use them.

Models. Creating a three-dimensional model as an end product should not be thought of as simply an opportunity for the children to practice manual skills. Making a model can involve using a great deal of information collected during the course of the project. For example, as part of a project on railways, a group of nine-year-olds made models of railway engines at four points in history. Some of their work was simply based on pictures they had found in books, but for each model they also had to read about the engines in order to get some details correct. The completed models were an excellent demonstration of their reading comprehension. In another project, some ten-year-olds made a model of their school buildings. This involved a great deal of measurement, consulting of plans, and rough sketching.

In both these examples children had to absorb and understand information from a variety of sources before putting it to use to construct their models. If all the children had done with the information was to write it down, their level of understanding would have been much lower.

With such a range of formats available for presenting information found during project work, and with such a variety of audiences to bear in mind, it is clear that there is no need for children simply to copy sections from reference books. Coping with the demands of presentation is a powerful learning experience in its own right.

. . . .

THE ROLE OF THE

TEACHER

There are many facets to the teacher's role during project work, encompassing activities from direct teaching of the whole class to deliberate withdrawal. The most important point to bear in mind, though, is that the teacher should do a great deal more than sit back and allow children to "get on with it." There is certainly a temptation for teachers to think that, having prepared the ground and helped children sort out goals for their work and plan how they will proceed, the children's own motivation will be sufficient to see them through. Indeed, many teachers will testify that a classful of children busily working with enthusiasm on their projects seems to need little attention. Teachers are thereby free to do other things, such as holding conferences with individual children about their reading or withdrawing small groups for extra help in basic skills. However, if this is the teacher's *only* role in project work, then a great deal of potential is being lost. It is crucial to realize that because children are highly motivated, this provides the very best context in which they can be taught many skills. The teacher should, therefore, have a clear teaching role during project work.

Sometimes this role does involve the teacher stepping back and allowing children's work to proceed for a time without intervention. All learners, adults and children alike, learn best when they themselves see the need to learn. Children doing project work that interests them will often find at some point that there are things they want badly to do but do not know how. In the right kind of environment, they should be able to ask their teacher for help. Their subsequent learning becomes much more effective because they have identified their own learning needs. Clearly, then, the teacher will be acting at times as a consultant rather than the director of children's work. This use of what has been called "skillful neglect" can, of course, be very difficult for teachers since it may mean watching children make mistakes without responding until the problems become apparent to the children themselves.

This is not to say that the teacher cannot structure occasions to lead children to see the need for learning something. This can be done as the teacher and children are planning the project by suggesting activities that are likely to give rise to children asking for help.

The teacher's primary roles in project work will therefore be as consultant, poser of problems, facilitator, and helper. Although the teacher can influence these things, they essentially depend on initiatives from the children. Of course, in addition to these roles the teacher also must be a *teacher*, who at many times during the project will wish to teach the children directly. This may involve teaching particular content or particular skills.

In what follows I discuss both direct teaching and the teacher's more responsive roles. Throughout I offer suggestions about ways teachers can encourage children to become more independent in their work.

Direct Teaching

GROUPING FOR INSTRUCTION

When the teacher feels some direct teaching is needed during a project, the basic organizational question to be sorted out is that of grouping. Sometimes it may be appropriate to treat the class as a whole and conduct class lessons on particular topics. At other times it may be preferable to teach the class a group at a time. Sometimes not all students will require this teaching, and it can be focused on particular groups. Finally, it may sometimes be appropriate to teach individuals. Some examples will clarify things.

In a project on vacations, one class of nine-year-olds was basically organized in groups, although each group had more or less the same tasks. Project planning was done by the whole class together. During the project all the students were brought together several times for class lessons. In one they were shown slides of several vacation resorts in different countries and discussed the special features of each. In this session the teacher was able to impart information he hoped would be reinforced by the children's own investigations in books and brochures. Another class lesson was spent discussing advertising techniques. First they read extracts from travel brochures and discussed how the writers made people want to visit the places described. This was extended to other advertisements, and later the students tried writing their own descriptions for an imaginary destination. This lesson took place shortly before the children were to begin designing their own brochures for their chosen resorts. In a third lesson, the teacher distributed passport application forms to each child. He went through the forms with the class and all the children filled one in. This lesson was not planned originally as a whole class activity; children were supposed to fill in these forms as part of their group and individual work. However, the teacher had noticed that the first few children to try this became very confused, so he decided to address it as a class lesson.

It can be seen from these examples that class lessons can focus on content, on preparing children to use skills they will need in the near future, and on skills with which children have already had some difficulties.

In another project, a class of eight-year-olds was following-up a reading of *Charlotte's Web*, and this resulted in work across several areas of the curriculum. Children were organized into groups and part of their work on the project involved each group preparing a booklet or poster on subtopics such as farmyard animals, spiders, the fairground, and so on. The rest of the project was done on a class and individual basis, with each child having a record sheet of work to be done. Class lessons were organized, but these tended to serve as stimuli for creative writing and poetry. More teaching was done on a group basis. For example, the group doing work on farmyard animals was shown some slides on this topic, while the rest of the class pursued other work. One group was introduced to curve stitching, and these children went on to make spider webs. This same group were told the story of Arachne, again while the rest of the class did other things. Another group was given a lesson on using a reference book after their teacher noticed that the children did not seem to know about the index pages.

The teaching in these examples focused on the specific needs of groups. Several individuals within the class were also given direct teaching, mostly on such things as using reference books or finding books in the library.

In both these examples, the basic grouping structure used by the teacher was to allow students to work alongside their friends.

There are, of course, alternative strategies, each of which has a role to play. Sometimes students might be grouped according to ability and levels of expertise. This will make direct teaching of the group easier, as it means the level of the teaching can be more narrowly focused. At other times mixed-ability groups might be used deliberately. This makes peer tutoring possible as an instructional strategy. The key point about grouping is to allow sufficient flexibility to enable a range of goals to be met.

INCIDENTAL TEACHING

One of the biggest points in favor of project work is that it provides a context that is interesting and meaningful to children in which a whole range of skills can be taught. This sort of teaching can help children see the purpose of these skills, and because they want to succeed in their project they are more likely to work hard at acquiring the know-how to help them do so. I refer to this teaching as "incidental" because it takes place as a sideline to the main work. This does not mean it is less important or that it cannot be planned for and, indeed, built into the project. As part of negotiation at the planning stage, the teacher can deliberately include activities that will provide opportunities for incidental teaching.

Let's return to the project on vacations, during which incidental teaching occurred a number of times. Among the teacher's aims for this project were the improvement of children's abilities to use reference books and the introduction of telephone directories. During the planning stage he made sure that activities involving appropriate skills were included in the project. He also made sure he had suitable resources available for when teaching would be done. These resources included six copies (borrowed from other classes and two public libraries) of one reference book on countries and several copies of the local Yellow Pages directory.

At the stage in the project when children were consulting reference books, the teacher was particularly alert for problems. When he noticed several children who were obviously not sure about things, he drew them together into a group. This happened twice, with two groups of six children. With each group he talked about finding information in books and asked how they would do it. Most of the children could tell him what they should do, even though he had observed that they had not actually been doing it. He gave out the reference books and suggested they play a game with them. This involved the teacher calling out topics and names and the children racing to be the first to find these in the book. They soon learned that it was quicker to use the index. This game was repeated on two further occasions to ensure the idea had been mastered.

Later in the project a group of children was planning how to obtain travel brochures. They knew they had to go to travel agents but did not know where the travel agents were in their town. The teacher at this point introduced the Yellow Pages and explained that these would help. The group found the travel agents' listing with the help of the teacher, who then suggested playing a game with the directories. He gave them some problems—"Help, my washing machine has broken down. Who can I call?"or "I've forgotten my wife's birthday. Where can I buy some flowers after school?"—which each child had to try to be the first to solve. This game subsequently became very popular with the class as a whole, and several children wrote what they called "Help!" cards for use in the game.

When the children had obtained plenty of brochures, the teacher suggested they each choose one particular trip and fill in the reservation form at the back of the brochure. This gave rise to a great deal of incidental work. One group was given a lesson on how to write their and their family's dates of birth. The whole class had to perform the calculations as they worked out the cost of their vacation. They were also given a valuable lesson on reading for details, as they had to read the small print of the brochures to find out exactly what the cost of a holiday would be. They discussed such things as insurance and discounts for children, and later marked the resorts they had chosen on maps, along with the airports they would fly from and to.

Only part of this work was fully planned at the beginning of the project, and clearly the first requirement of a teacher contemplating this approach is to be alert and prepared for teaching opportunities. There is little point in noticing an opportunity for incidental teaching if you must wait a day or two to gather appropriate resources. The whole point of this approach is that the children understand why they are doing a certain exercise: because it will help them do better at something they want to do. The immediacy of the moment is all important.

Facilitating Learning

Children, like adults, learn by doing. As stated at the beginning of this chapter, teachers need to be prepared to stay at the sidelines sometimes, allowing children to proceed on their own. This does not mean doing nothing, however. There are other more responsive roles the teacher needs to consider during project work. These have to do with the ways the teacher can be organized to ensure involvement and increase independence in children as they pursue their project work.

ENSURING CHILDREN' S INVOLVEMENT

For the teacher, one of the challenges of project work, which involves children in following their own initiatives and in doing a large variety of tasks at different times, is that of making sure everyone has the opportunity to

— take part in discussion of aims and help make plans
— have experience of as wide a range of tasks as possible.

There are some techniques that can help with this.

Keeping records. Evaluating and keeping records of children's achievements in project work is discussed more fully in the next chapter. At this point, however, it should be noted that recording each child's achievement can, by itself, act as a check on children's experiences. If we record that a child has developed a certain skill, that must mean that he or she has had experience of that skill. If we can make no record, then the child's experience has been lacking. So record keeping can alert us to gaps in experience.

Although indications of experience would necessarily appear on an evaluative record, we might also keep a record specifically of experience. This could be particularly valuable for experiences that tend not to be assessed in the way that, say, reading and mathematics skills are. Such a record might include painting, drawing, using clay, making a collage design, model making, using the tape recorder, drama, mime, interviewing, cooking, weaving, and so on. A record of these experiences could be a simple grid of activities and children's names, with a tick being recorded for every activity individual children had experience of during a project. Gaps could be compensated for in future activities.

Rotating roles. A deliberate policy could be followed whereby important roles such as group leader, group reporter, member of editorial board for the class magazine, etc., were rotated so that, over a period, every child in the class had a turn at each role.

In addition, the duties involved in each role could be such that every child would have experience of various types of responsibility. Group leaders, for example, could be responsible for allocation of particular tasks within their group, although they would have to take group members' opinions into account. They would also keep a record of the progress of each activity. The example of such a record, used in a class project on communications, was prepared by a group doing work on television.

Job	Whose job?	Completed
Graph of favorite TV programs	Darren, Gary	
Analysis of TV schedule	Susan, Lee	
Wall chart design and mounting	Avril, Gary	
TV camera section	David, Susan	
History section	Lee, Darren	
Program section	Avril, Gary	
Stars section	David, Susan	

The group reporter could be responsible for reporting back to the class on the group's progress with their project. Members of the editorial board would be responsible for the design, collation, and production of the class project magazine.

Spreading specialists. One of the common features of project work is that children with specialist skills tend to get asked to use these a great deal of the time. So, for example, children good at art tend to get to do most of the important artwork, especially if it is intended to be put on display. Likewise, children good at using the computer tend to do this a lot. As mentioned in an earlier chapter, this is undesirable, even though it might produce good results. First, it deprives other children of opportunities to practice the things that specialists do. And second, the skilled children themselves are deprived of opportunities to try other things. Asking these children to fill the consultancy role described previously is a good way of addressing these problems.

Part of any teacher's task is to help children become sufficiently independent to function on their own. This particularly applies in project work. Finding information and doing something with it are common enough tasks for adults, who do not have teachers beside them to offer guidance. So children have ultimately to learn to pursue projects independently of a teacher.

There is a good deal that teachers can do during project work to move children along the road to independence. Many ideas have been dealt with in previous chapters. Especially important is encouraging children to share in goal setting and project planning. Children can't learn to make decisions about their actions if they are not given the opportunity to make some. Also important is giving responsibility for certain parts of the project to specific children. Again, nobody can learn to have responsibility if he or she is never given any. Of course, these strategies will not always work. Children are children and they will sometimes get things wrong, fail to live up to the responsibility they are given, let others down. This is the way of the world. But this fact is not sufficient reason for not attempting to make children more independent. There is a large element of faith necessary here on the part of the teacher.

There are other things teachers can do to encourage independence which perhaps go somewhat against the grain, but can be clearly justified. These include refusing to help children do things you think they should be doing for themselves—such as showing them where in a book the item they require is, or spelling out words for them. Being independent is harder work than being helped, and it is important that children should not simply take the easy way out by asking their teacher. This does not mean never helping children. The teacher is, after all, there to teach. But sometimes being too ready to help can actually teach children unproductive things. After a short time of this attitude from their teacher, even quite young children are capable of surprising independence.

It is fairly obvious that, if this view of project work is taken, the teacher is going to be occasionally disappointed with the quality of the products that emerge. It must be remembered that the main learning in project work is in the process of doing it, and so the product is of secondary importance. However, it will sometimes be necessary to convince outsiders (such as parents) that standards are not slipping because, for example, a child-designed wall chart might have some spelling mistakes and not be perfectly mounted.

One way to avoid some of the problem of inadequate products is to develop students' abilities to monitor their own work. Specific techniques for doing this will be discussed in more detail in the next chapter. At this point I will note only that self-monitoring needs to be built into the project from the beginning, and that the project should be organized with this in mind.

If, for example, one of the strategies adopted is to have regular sessions at which groups report back on their progress through the project, then these sessions need to be planned for within the time allocated to the project. Children will also need to be taught what is expected from them in these sessions, and how to give reports. This probably means that time will need to be allocated for the teacher to discuss each group's report with them. This then is yet another extension to the teacher's role during project work.

The teacher clearly has many roles during project work, and the variations in what he or she might be doing can often cause some confusion. Forward planning is important for ensuring maximum teaching effect during projects, but you must be prepared to deviate from plans in the light of circumstances. Be prepared also to adopt the skillful-neglect role referred to earlier. Students can only learn to be independent when given the space to try.

EVALUATING THE PROJECT

Clearly, if we are to claim that teaching through projects is an effective means of instruction, we need to be able to demonstrate this effectiveness. This means that we need to be able to evaluate project work and, more especially, students' achievements in projects and their development in various areas.

Of course, evaluation does not only serve as a means of justifying what teachers do; it also provides valuable information on which to base future teaching. By assessing students in their project work, teachers can plan activities to build on strengths and achievements and to remedy weaknesses.

Evaluation has, therefore, both an accountability function and a diagnostic one. Bearing these in mind, teachers need to select appropriate techniques with which to evaluate students' progress in the various skills they use in project work. This chapter makes some suggestions in this area. First, I discuss what exactly teachers might evaluate in their students' project work, and then I go on to look at particular methods of evaluation. Evaluation, like every other aspect of project work, can be designed to involve the students more than is perhaps usual, and possibilities for ways of doing this are also suggested. Finally, the issue of record keeping is discussed, and I offer a record sheet that can be adapted as necessary.

What to Evaluate

The question of what to evaluate in project work obviously relates back to what the aims of this work were in the first place. As I discussed in the first chapter, there are three broad categories for the goals teachers might have in any project: the development of knowledge and concepts, skills, and attitudes. These areas also provide a structure for what to evaluate, although each project will be slightly different in the emphasis it places on each area. These areas cause slightly different problems when it comes to evaluation.

KNOWLEDGE AND CONCEPTS

I stated quite forcibly in the opening chapter that the acquisition of factual knowledge is really a minor aim in project work. As the students will be well motivated to find out about the topic, this type of learning can almost be taken for granted. What cannot be taken for granted, however, is their development of understanding of a variety of concepts. A concept is usually held to be a kind of knowledge that becomes generalizable. Thus, students studying English history may learn, for example, about life in Norman, Tudor, and Victorian times, and from this knowledge build up generalized concepts about historical change. Similarly, they may observe that water changes when boiled or frozen, that paper changes when burned, and that an iron nail changes when left in the damp. From this knowledge they may build up concepts about chemical and physical change and, from these two related sets of ideas, develop more generalized concepts about the nature of change and of cause and effect. Clearly understanding these concepts requires knowledge and practical experience, but it also requires—or at least is considerably accelerated by—discussion and teaching that enables students to see links more clearly. This is far more important than any particular bits of knowledge that may be encountered. Yes, concepts are formed by generalizations from knowledge and experience, but not from only certain pieces of knowledge or only particular experiences. The concept of change, for example, may be built up from any number of different experiences of change, and these experiences can be built into any project, whatever the subject.

The evaluation of concept development is much more difficult than the evaluation of students' knowledge. Knowledge can be assessed simply by asking students questions—although there is no guarantee, of course, that this knowledge is permanent. Concepts, on the other hand, are internal understandings that can only be assessed indirectly. Another complication here is the need for a sort of "pre-assessment." If teachers are to provide appropriate teaching to assist concept development, they need to be aware of the stages their students have already reached. This demands some form of evaluation even before the project is begun.

More open to assessment, since they relate to what students actually do, are the skills that may develop through project work. In the opening chapter, I divided skills into four categories: investigation, practical, information, and communication. Each of these can be evaluated, although some will need a more indirect approach than others.

Investigation skills include observing, identifying, classifying, recording, and explaining. Because of their nature these skills will be used in practical situations where students are finding out at first hand, rather than using books or other sources of information. They are therefore impossible to assess in situations that are not practical. This means evaluation requires the use of observation techniques rather than construction of an artificial assessment instrument.

Practical skills form an extremely wide area. Particular projects will involve the use of different ones. Three subareas described earlier were

— skills involved in arts and crafts
— skills involved in using particular pieces of equipment
— skills involved in presenting work.

With the exception of those in the last category, the development of these skills tends not to be evaluated very often, or very closely. Many teachers will classify their students as "good [or not] at arts and crafts," but few will be more specific and identify particular strengths and weaknesses. This may be because these skills are not felt to be so important, because they are difficult to assess, or because they are widely regarded as not really amenable to teaching. Only the second of these reasons has much truth in it. Being able to express ideas, in whatever medium, is a very valuable asset, and is certainly not exclusively an ability one is either born with or not. It is, however, difficult to assess, since the tendency is to judge simply from the product that emerges. A more sophisticated assessment takes into account the context in which something is produced, and the facilities and resources available to help produce it.

Information and study skills were defined earlier as defining a subject and purpose, and locating, selecting, organizing, evaluating, and communicating information.

Evaluating the development of these skills is trickier than is often imagined. Many of us might think that all we need to do to assess whether students can find information in a book or choose the correct piece of information to answer a particular question is ask them. However, it is possible, and indeed quite common, for students to be able to give the correct answers to questions of this sort but use quite different and less efficient strategies when left to themselves to do actual tasks. Several investigations have found this discrepancy between what students say they would do in looking for information and what they actually do. Because of this, the only way to really evaluate mastery of these skills is to watch students using them in real situations.

Communication skills are obviously used throughout the elementary curriculum, rather than just in project work. However, talking, listening, reading, and writing are at the core of project work, and their development needs to be evaluated within its context as well as in other situations. These skills, especially reading and writing, have traditionally been assessed more than any other through formal tests. The problems of this approach will be discussed later, but at this point it should be mentioned that communication skills are tools, and as such need to be assessed as they are being used to perform real tasks. Project work certainly provides tasks that require these tools, and so assessment can take place within this element of the curriculum.

ATTITUDES

The assessment of students' attitudes is more difficult than that of any other area. Finding out what students really feel about things, rather than what they say they feel, poses enormous problems. Any evaluation method has its weaknesses, and it may be that teachers will need to be satisfied with a best estimate. Yet if helping students develop positive attitudes to school work and to one another are worthwhile goals of project work, some way, however unreliable, needs to be found to tell if these goals are being achieved. Students' attitudes to learning, their curiosity, their ability and willingness to work independently, and their attitudes to cooperating with others are all things project work is capable of improving. Evaluation is needed to inform teachers whether this is actually happening.

Methods of Evaluation

A common reaction to talk of evaluation and assessment is to think in terms of testing students. Discussion of methods of evaluation then becomes a search for the right test to use. The debate on the role of testing is much wider than the scope of this book but, with special reference to project work, several points can be made that may also have a bearing on other areas of the curriculum.

The first point is that there are actually very few published tests that claim to assess most of the skills developed in project work. There are tests for reading of course, but only one or two limited tests for information skills and, as far as I am aware, none for investigation skills. It might be possible to produce tests to check students' memories of facts encountered in projects, but it is clearly almost impossible to produce a test of conceptual development, which is far more important. By and large, if teachers require tests for project work, they will have to devise their own.

The second and perhaps most important point is that if a test were found and administered, it would probably reveal very little about students' abilities to pursue project work or what they had learned through doing it. The test might indicate what they were capable of doing on that test, but that would not necessarily be the same as what they were capable of doing in a different situation. Because test taking tends to be stressful for students, the results might not even reveal a child's true capabilities on that test. Test situations are, by their very nature, artificial, and their results are a very unreliable guide to real capabilities.

You might think this was a serious problem but, fortunately, the fact that tests are unreliable as a means of evaluating project work does not really matter. There are other basic ways of assessing students' performance during such work:

— looking at what students produce
— observing students while they are working
— asking students questions about what they are doing.

These methods all evaluate students' performance while they are actually doing projects. The work itself is used as a testing situation, and so evaluations are that much more reliable a guide to real abilities.

ASSESSING PRODUCTS

It may seem that I am contradicting myself by suggesting that end products be evaluated when I have stressed throughout this book that, in project work, the process is more important than the product. I have to admit, however, that there are several clues to students' achievements that can be gleaned from a careful inspection of their work. If this is combined with other assessment techniques that focus more on the process of project work, then a rounded evaluation can be built up.

Four particular considerations must be kept in mind when assessing products:

1. Products cannot be judged without taking the aims of the project into account.
2. The assessment must also take into consideration students' differing capabilities. A piece of work may be good for one child but well below another's capacity.
3. The assessment should also focus on whether the work is appropriate for its intended audience. The only real way of judging this is to give the work to the intended audience for whatever kind of evaluation is feasible.
4. Finally, the assessment should take into account the context in which the work was produced. This includes such things as the resources available to the child, the kind of help he or she received, and the time taken to produce this outcome.

Let's look at this kind of assessment in action. As part of a project on the environment, Christopher and Julie, two nine-year-olds, read pamphlets from the World Wildlife Fund and Friends of the Earth about the threat of extinction to certain animal species. After discussion with their teacher, they (along with four other students) agreed to write their own pamphlets about this problem, which would have the aim not only of giving its readers information but also of encouraging them to take action. These readers were to be other students in the same class.

The texts of Christopher's and Julie's pamphlets appear on pages 88-89. Clearly only Christopher's work really fulfills the original aim. It is written in a very direct style that communicates information but also tries to worry its readers. Julie's piece conveys information but seems to lack commitment and has a style too bland to have real impact.

Christopher's Pamphlet

The Wld Wildlife Fund

all over the world people are killing and skinning animals. Some animals like the elephants are being killed for there ivory tusks. other animals tigers for instance are being killed for the beautiful skins, for bags coats and other things. Whales are killed for dog meat, and perfumes this has been done so many times that the whale has almost become extinct in the past your whales have been killed for the oily skin.

The eagle is queit rare it is sometimes found in Scotland. Hunters get to hunt for eagles and steel there eggs. they has the eggs blown & then sell then this happens to lots of birds and this is the cause of the birds becoming rare. Also of the eggs and lots of the birds eggs are stellen so the eggs can not hatch into chicks.

When looking at these products in terms of the students' differing abilities, the teacher noted that Christopher was a boy who rarely shone in school work. From his conversation it was clear that he was bright and interested in a wide range of things, but the work he produced was invariably slipshod and rarely finished. This piece was one of his very best, and the teacher praised it as such. Julie, on the other hand, almost always excelled in her work. She was extremely conscientious and was regarded as clever by all the teachers in the school. This piece was fairly typical of her work: reasonably tidy and accurate, but not inspired.

Both pieces were then read by the intended audience of other students in the class. When choosing work for the class display on the project, the students included the first but not the second. They commented that the first piece "made them angry," but insisted that Christopher word-process it before putting it into the display, because "other children won't be able to read it."

As a final consideration in assessing these pamphlets, the teacher noted that both students had similar resources available to them for their work. The pieces were actually written within one lesson and were first drafts, but neither child wished to revise.

The obvious difficulty with a piece of work like Christopher's is that it has to be read very carefully before its merits are appreciated. It is easy to be put off by the poor presentation and bad spelling and not to realize that this is, in fact, a remarkable piece of writing. Writing like Julie's will often be judged more kindly because it is neater and more accurate, but this is really a much more ordinary piece. By assessing the two pieces within a set of established criteria and guidelines, the teacher reached this conclusion readily and was able to give both Julie and Christopher appropriate feedback.

OBSERVING STUDENTS

Teachers observe students working all the time. As a result of this observation we make assessments of students' abilities and attitudes, and plan future work. Yet when asked about their assessment methods, teachers hardly ever count observation among them. Perhaps because it is so common an activity and seems so subjective, we underrate its potential for providing assessment information. Its greatest strength lies in the fact that it enables teachers to make assessments while students are actually working on their projects, and does not require them to be withdrawn into a special testing situation.

To use observation deliberately as an assessment technique requires a systematic approach. It also requires some means of recording the information gained, rather than relying on memory. A systematic approach involves first of all knowing exactly what you are looking for. This might mean deciding on the skills you hope to assess and preparing a checklist of them. An alternative approach is to list the activities students will be doing, leaving space to note observations about their performance. The figure gives an example of a simple checklist for making evaluations of reading and information skills.

A Checklist to Assess Reading and Information Skills

Skill	Points to look for	Performance assessment
Setting goals	Can student specify goals for the work to be undertaken? Can student specify an audience for the final outcome?	
Defining specific purposes	Can student set questions for investigation? Can student organize his/her work?	
Locating information	Can student find sources of information? Can student use these sources effectively?	
Using books	Can student assess appropriate books? Can student find information in books?	
Using appropriate reading strategy	Can student skim, scan, and understand what is read?	
Using information	Can student take notes? Can student present information effectively?	
Evaluation of work	Can student evaluate his/her work? Can student suggest ways to improve the work?	

The problem of applying such checklists still remains. Clearly they cannot be used for observing all the students in a class at once. Neither is it sensible simply to rely on remembering things worthy of note, committing them to paper when time permits after the event. A systematic approach needs to be devised to ensure that regular observations are made of each child.

One way of doing this is to focus on two or three students only each day. Over two or three weeks the whole class can be covered, and the process begins again. This is clearly not ideal, since some useful information about students' abilities is bound to be missed. The system does ensure, however, that all students and all specified skills are given regular attention.

ASKING QUESTIONS

Simply observing what students do is not really sufficient to evaluate how they are thinking about their tasks. A way of penetrating into this is to ask them questions about how they performed various tasks or what they were thinking about as they did them. Three types of questions are useful for this.

Looking back questions are of the "Can you tell me how you did that?" type. They are most appropriate when you are looking at a student's work with her. Answers may be more revealing if questions are phrased in these sorts of ways:

— That's very interesting. Where did you find that out?
— What a lot of information! How did you manage to find it all so quickly?
— Now, you used the encyclopedia here. Can you tell me what you did?

Looking forward questions are of the "Can you tell me how you will do that?" type. They ask students to think about their actions before they do them. It is, of course, possible that because the question causes students to think through what they will do, they actually perform differently than they would have. The question then has a teaching role, as well as being a way of seeing whether they know what to do. Questions such as these may be useful:

— When you go to the library to look for that book, can you tell me what you will do?
— When you've got all the information, how will you organize it?
— Now, how will you be able to tell which books are useful for your project?

Thinking out loud questions are of the "What are you thinking as you are doing that?" type. They can help make students' thinking about certain tasks explicit and alert the teacher to faulty approaches. They may include questions such as

— Can you tell me why you're choosing those things to note from that book?
— That book seems quite hard. Can you tell me how you're managing to sort it out?

Involving the Students

As with other parts of project work, it is desirable and possible to involve students in evaluating their own work. If students evaluate themselves it is more likely that they will realize where they need to improve, and this realization will make them more likely actually to improve.

Most students will not of their own accord make very detailed evaluations of their work. They need to be encouraged and led into ways of doing this. One very effective technique is to ask them regularly how they performed various tasks, and encourage them to say whether they would do things differently the next time. Approaches such as the following might be used:

— Now, you have found a lot out about the invention of television, and you've used several books. Do you think you could have done that any quicker?
— You've finished your poster now. If you were starting all over again, do you think you would do it exactly the same way? Or would you do some things differently?
— Your group has been working together on a model of the airport. Do you think you worked well as a group? How might you have organized things differently, do you think?

After some guidance from the teacher, students might eventually be able to ask one another questions like this.

Another technique is to ask children deliberately for evaluations of their own finished work, whether individual items or complete projects. This can be done informally by simply asking them questions, or they can write a few sentences about what they think of their work. This can be open-ended ("How would you rate your presentation? Why?") or more structured ("Think of three things you are really pleased about in this work and three things that might be improved").

When students are thoroughly at home with the idea of critiquing their own work, they can be asked to offer evaluations of other students', perhaps working in small groups. Care needs to be taken so that criticisms do not become too negative or damage other students' self-esteem. If the task is phrased in such a way that it asks students to note positive aspects and suggest ways the work might be improved, rather than simply saying what is wrong with it, destructive criticism can be minimized.

Another self-evaluation technique is the regular report-back session suggested earlier. This might involve one child from each group giving a brief report to the rest of the class on how the group's project work is progressing. The reporter can be encouraged to mention any problems the group has had, anything they are particularly proud of, or any areas in which they are not sure how to proceed and would really like to have some help. The group's problems could then be discussed by the whole class, and suggestions made as to how they might be overcome. In this way, a cooperative atmosphere can be established.

Record Keeping

The final aspect of evaluation of project work is that of keeping records of students' progress. Teachers are regularly told, of course, that they should keep records of progress in all areas of the curriculum. The golden rule of record keeping, however, is simply this: If records are not consulted and used as a guide for future teaching, then there was no point in making them in the first place.

Teachers, of course, have a limited amount of time available to them. Records must therefore be economic in terms of the time needed to compile them, and also to consult and draw on them. Because of this, most schools and teachers adopt quick, checklist-type records, or records requiring only one- or two-word comments.

As far as project work is concerned, there are two types of record which are useful. The first records the experiences and areas students have covered, and the second is a record of their development in particular areas.

In the second chapter I suggested that the problem of continuity in project work might be alleviated by keeping records of the areas students have covered and the major experiences they have had within these. This would avoid a child doing a project on, say, dinosaurs for three years running without any of his teachers being aware of this repetition. If a teacher knew the projects students had already covered, he might still choose to repeat—and extend—any of them, but this would be done with deliberate purpose rather than accidentally. A simple record such as Darren Taylor's might accompany individual students through the school.

An Experience Record

Name: Darren Taylor	Year: Junior 2
Project	**Major activities**
Vikings	Story writing, drama, model-making, using reference books, map-making.
Water	Science experiments, collage, editor of class magazine, visit to reservoir, designed school questionnaire.

ACHIEVEMENT RECORDS

Records of students' development in various areas need to run alongside their experience records. These may take two forms. First, the teacher needs to make a record for her own use. This should be fairly detailed so that she will be able to use it as a basis for planning work for the students in the class. Although simple forms of recording information will probably have to be adopted—for example, checkmarks or crosses, or classifications into "Good," "Average," or "Poor"—there is a lot to be gained by using more expanded forms if the time is available.

Second, there will need to be a record to pass on to the next teacher when a child changes class. This probably does not require the same level of detail, but will be more of a summary of the main strengths and weaknesses of the child. Darren's achievement record is an example of this second kind.

An Achievement Record

Name: —Darren Taylor	Year: —Junior 2
Area	**Comment on progress**
Investigation skills	Able to observe quite carefully and discuss and classify observations. Recording still rather weak.
Practical	Presentation quite poor. Excellent design.
Information	Use of reference books improving. Planning is good. More consideration needs to be given to presenting information.
Communication	Reading for information good. Can explain ideas well but has difficulty in written expression.
Attitudes	Very positive towards learning and information. Co-operates well, but needs help to become more independent in his work.
General conceptual development	Has begun to understand historical change. Needs more experience to grasp cause and effect, especially in science work. Finds it difficult to approach tasks systematically.